Elementary Operations and
Optimal Derivations

D1526220

Linguistic Inquiry Monographs
Samuel Jay Keyser, general editor

Elementary Operations and
Optimal Derivations

Hisatsugu Kitahara

The MIT Press
Cambridge, Massachusetts
London, England

© 1997 Massachusetts Institute of Technology

All rights reserved. No part of this book may be reproduced in any form by any electronic or mechanical means (including photocopying, recording, or information storage and retrieval) without permission in writing from the publisher.

This book was set in Times Roman by Asco Trade Typesetting Ltd., Hong Kong. Printed and bound in the United States of America.

Library of Congress Cataloging-in-Publication Data

Kitahara, Hisatsugu.
 Elementary operations and optimal derivations / Hisatsugu Kitahara.
   p.   cm.—(Linguistic inquiry monographs ; 31)
 Includes bibliographical references and index.
 ISBN 0-262-11222-1.—ISBN 0-262-61129-5 (pbk.)
  1. Generative grammar. 2. Minimalist theory (Linguistics). I. Title. II. Series.
P158.K58   1997
415—dc20   96-36404
                                                              CIP

To my parents, Teruhisa and Yukiko Kitahara,
and to my brothers, Terumasa and Tadashi

Contents

Series Foreword

We are pleased to present the thirty-first in the series *Linguistic Inquiry Monographs*. These monographs present new and original research beyond the scope of the article. We hope they will benefit our field by bringing to it perspectives that will stimulate further research and insight.

Originally published in limited editions, the *Linguistic Inquiry Monographs* are now more widely available. This change is due to the great interest engendered by the series and by the needs of a growing readership. The editors thank the readers for their support and welcome suggestions about future directions for the series.

Samuel Jay Keyser
for the Editorial Board

Acknowledgments

I am indebted to a number of people for their generous assistance with this project.

First and foremost, I am grateful to Samuel D. Epstein for his continuing guidance. He has listened to virtually every analysis produced during this investigation. His insightful comments have broadened my perspectives on theoretical linguistics. His helpful suggestions have provided me with a number of new approaches (if not solutions) to linguistic phenomena confronting this investigation.

I am also deeply grateful to Noam Chomsky for his invaluable help. His challenging questions and criticisms have set a number of higher objectives for this investigation. Working with him has been rewarding and a great privilege.

For listening to every major idea presented in this work, I would like to thank Howard Lasnik, Mamoru Saito, and Höskuldur Thráinsson. Many new ideas have emerged from their responses.

I am grateful to Chris Collins, Henry Davis, Marcel den Dikken, Robert Freidin, Günther Grewendorf, Masayuki Oishi, Michael Rochemont, and two anonymous reviewers for their extensive comments and suggestions on this work.

I thank Eric Rosen for his comments and his assistance in the final preparation of the manuscript. I am also indebted to Anne Mark for invaluable editorial improvements too numerous to mention.

I would like to extend my thanks to the following people for their various contributions: Jun Abe, Rose-Marie Déchaine, Hamida Demirdache, Scott Ferguson, Erich Groat, Dianne Jonas, Yasuhiko Kato, Masatoshi Koizumi, John O'Neil, Geoff Poole, Isaiah Teshima, Shigeo Tonoike, and Jan-Wouter Zwart.

Finally, I am most indebted to Ruriko Kawashima, who has listened to all the ideas, often incomplete, developed during this undertaking. I thank her for her patience and for her unfailing feedback. Without her support and encouragement, this work would never have reached this stage.

Much of the basis for this study is presented in my doctoral dissertation, "Target α: A Unified Theory of Movement and Structure-Building" (completed at Harvard University in May 1994). I would like to express my gratitude for the support I received from the Department of Linguistics at Harvard University.

Special gratitude goes to the following three institutions where this research project was conducted: the Department of Linguistics and Philosophy at Massachusetts Institute of Technology (fall 1994), the Program in Linguistics at Princeton University (spring 1995), and the Department of Linguistics at the University of British Columbia (1995–96).

The material in this monograph benefited from very lively discussion in my seminar "Economy and Minimalism," conducted at the University of British Columbia in 1995, and from presentations at the University of Lund (the 16th Generative Linguists in the Old World Colloquium), the University of Maryland at College Park, Massachusetts Institute of Technology (the 1st Conference on Formal Approaches to Japanese Linguistics), Meiji Gakuin University, Sophia University, Princeton University, Harvard University, Michigan State University, the University of Michigan, and the University of British Columbia. An earlier version of part of chapter 2 appeared in *Linguistic Inquiry* 26.1.

The research reported here was supported in part by a Mrs. Giles Whiting Fellowship at Harvard University (1993–94), an Izaak Walton Killam Postdoctoral Fellowship at the University of British Columbia (1995–96), and a research fellowship from Green College at the University of British Columbia (1995–96). I am grateful to each institution for its generous support.

Introduction

This study, conducted within the Minimalist Program outlined in Chomsky 1991, 1993, and further elaborated in Chomsky 1994, 1995, is primarily concerned with the *elementary operations* of the computational system C_{HL} for human language and with the principles of Universal Grammar (UG) that constrain derivations generated by C_{HL}. The elementary operations of C_{HL} are *concatenation* and *replacement*. The proposal that these are indeed the elementary operations allows disparate syntactic operations to be unified. The principles of UG are divided into two groups: *economy principles*, which determine what counts as an *optimal* derivation among competitors, and *computational principles*, which determine what counts as a *legitimate step* in a given derivation.

Articulating the interaction between the elementary operations of C_{HL} and the principles of UG, this study determines the set of optimal derivations involving only legitimate steps and demonstrates how these derivations characterize, without stipulation, a number of linguistic expressions that have long occupied the center of syntactic investigation. Many of the conditions empirically motivated by such linguistic expressions and assumed to be axiomatic within previous analyses are thus shown to be eliminable.

This study is presented in four chapters. Chapter 1 outlines a minimalist view of language design in which the guiding ideas and relevant assumptions of the Minimalist Program are reviewed.

Chapter 2 concerns the syntactic operations of C_{HL}: *Merge, Move,* and *Erase.* I argue that these seemingly discrete operations are unifiable in terms of more elementary operations of *concatenation* and *replacement* (in the spirit of Lasnik and Saito's (1992) *Affect* α hypothesis). Given this unified structure-building analysis, I propose that economy of derivation constrains the elementary operations of concatenation and replacement.

More specifically, I revise the formulation of the *Shortest Derivation Condition* (SDC), "Minimize the number of operations necessary for convergence" (Chomsky 1991, 1993; Epstein 1992), as "Minimize the number of *elementary* operations necessary for convergence." As an immediate consequence of this seemingly minor but fundamental revision, the empirically desirable aspects of *strict cyclicity* are shown to be deducible. As a natural extension of this analysis, I also demonstrate that the empirical motivation for *Procrastinate*, an axiom governing the timing of verb movement, object shift, and expletive insertion, is explicable without any stipulation regarding pre- versus post-Spell-Out cost distinctions. The intuitive idea behind Procrastinate presented in Chomsky 1993 is also discussed in light of the (revised) SDC analysis.

In the appendix to chapter 2, I examine the timing of expletive insertion in *multiple-subject constructions* (MSCs) (Jonas 1995, 1996; Chomsky 1995). I argue that insertion of an expletive in the outer specifier of an MSC is ensured by convergence considerations. I demonstrate that a derivation D yielding the MSC with an expletive Exp crashes if D fails to insert Exp in the outer specifier of the MSC.

Chapter 3 examines a number of movement phenomena involving violations of *Relativized Minimality* (Rizzi 1990), the *Superiority Condition* (Chomsky 1973), and the *Proper Binding Condition* (Fiengo 1977; May 1977). Assuming that a derivation employing a greater number of illegitimate steps induces a greater degree of deviance (Chomsky 1965; Epstein 1990), I argue that the various contrasts exhibited by such movement phenomena, motivating these three seemingly distinct conditions, receive a unified analysis under minimalist assumptions. I demonstrate that the apparent diversity of these movement phenomena is illusory and epiphenomenal; in fact, it results from the computational principles of UG, in particular the *Minimal Link Condition* (MLC).

In the appendix to chapter 3, I extend the MLC analysis to German data involving unbound traces resulting from *short scrambling* and *topicalization* (Müller 1993, 1994) and to Japanese data involving unbound traces resulting from *long scrambling* (Saito 1989, 1992). I argue that the various contrasts exhibited by these movement phenomena are also deducible from the MLC analysis if scrambling and topicalization are instances of movement driven by morphological necessity.

Chapter 4 concerns degrees of deviance exhibited by derivations employing only one illegitimate step (violating the MLC). For example, *wh*-island violations resulting from the extraction of adjuncts, subjects, and so-called quasi objects are far more severe than *wh*-island violations resulting from the extraction of objects (see, among others, Chomsky 1986a; Cinque 1990; Epstein 1987, 1991; Huang 1982; Kayne 1984; Lasnik and Saito 1984, 1992; Manzini 1992; Rizzi 1990). To capture such asymmetries in deviance, I develop a chain formation analysis incorporating already existing, independently motivated Case-theoretic distinctions, under which the degrees of deviance exhibited by derivations involving only one illegitimate step (violating the MLC) are deducible from the condition of *Full Interpretation* (FI) applying at LF. I argue that a derivation employing one illegitimate step but yielding an LF representation satisfying FI is only marginally deviant. By contrast, a derivation similarly employing one illegitimate step but yielding an LF representation violating FI is, naturally, more severely deviant.

Chapter 1

A Minimalist View of
Language Design

This study is conducted within the Minimalist Program outlined in Chomsky 1991, 1993, and further elaborated in Chomsky 1994, 1995. This chapter briefly reviews the guiding ideas and relevant analyses presented there.[1]

1.1 A General Outlook

A particular language is an instance of the initial state of the *language faculty* with options specified. One component of the language faculty is a *generative procedure* (I-language; henceforth, language) that generates *structural descriptions* (SDs): pairs of representations (π, λ). π is a PF representation interpreted at the *articulatory-perceptual* (A-P) interface. λ is an LF representation interpreted at the *conceptual-intentional* (C-I) interface. A *grammar* is a theory of a particular language. *Universal Grammar* (UG) is a theory of the initial state of the relevant component of the language faculty. Under the *principles-and-parameters* model, the latest version of which is the Minimalist Program, UG provides a fixed system of principles and a finite array of finitely valued parameters.

The generative procedure consists of a *lexicon* and a *computational system*. The lexicon specifies lexical items (LIs) with their idiosyncratic properties. The computational system selects LIs from an array of lexical choices and generates derivations and SDs in accordance with the *computational principles* of UG (e.g., Last Resort) and the *economy principles* of UG (e.g., Shortest Derivation).

In generative grammar, it has been assumed that "languages are based on simple principles that interact to form often intricate structures" and that "the language faculty is nonredundant, in that particular phenomena are not 'overdetermined' by principles of language" (Chomsky 1993, 2).

The Minimalist Program takes these assumptions as a mode of inquiry and seeks a maximally simple design for language. Given this view, the linguistic levels are taken to be only those conceptually necessary—namely, PF and LF—meaning that there are no (intermediate) levels of D-Structure or S-Structure.[2]

A pair (π, λ) receives some interpretation at the relevant interface level if each representation satisfies the conditions imposed at the interface, which Chomsky (1994; 1995, 221) calls *bare output conditions*. A derivation *converges* if it yields such a pair (π, λ); otherwise, it *crashes*.

To be a linguistic expression, a pair (π, λ) must be formed by a derivation that is not only convergent but also *optimal* among its competitors, where optimality is determined by the economy principles of UG: less economical derivations are blocked even if they converge.[3]

In searching for a maximally simple design for language, the Minimalist Program proceeds with this general outlook.

1.2 The Generative Procedure

The generative procedure consists of a single lexicon (with limited lexical variety) and a single computational system C_{HL} for human language. C_{HL} derives a pair (π, λ), where π and λ consist of nothing beyond features of LIs, meaning that C_{HL} does no more than arrange lexical features, which Chomsky (1995, 225) calls a condition of *inclusiveness*.

A linguistic expression is a pair (π, λ) derived from the same lexical choices by an optimal convergent derivation. That is, C_{HL} maps some array of lexical choices to the pair (π, λ). The array of lexical choices is called a *numeration*: a set of pairs (LI, i). LI is an item of the lexicon and i is its index, understood to be the number of times that LI is selected. In mapping a numeration N to a pair (π, λ), C_{HL} selects an item from N and reduces its index by 1. This operation is called *Select*. A generating procedure does not count as a derivation unless all indices reduce to zero.

Given the numeration N, C_{HL} recursively constructs syntactic objects from LIs selected from N and syntactic objects already formed. The simplest such operation takes a pair of syntactic objects (SO_i, SO_j), constructs a new syntactic object SO_{ij}, and substitutes SO_{ij} for (SO_i, SO_j). This operation is called *Merge*. A derivation then converges only if Select and Merge have applied often enough to exhaust the initial numeration and yield a single syntactic object.

Another role of the numeration N is to fix the reference set for determining whether a derivation from N to a pair (π, λ) is optimal. In a given stage Σ of a derivation D, C_{HL} considers only continuations of D from Σ with the remaining parts of the numeration N and selects an operation applying to Σ that leads D to become the optimal convergent derivation (Chomsky 1994; 1995, 227).

A derivation yields a pair (π, λ), where π and λ are differently constituted: elements interpretable at PF are not interpretable at LF. At some point, then, C_{HL} splits a derivation into two parts: one forming π and the other forming λ. This operation is called *Spell-Out*. Given the structure Σ already constructed, Spell-Out applies to Σ and strips away from it those elements relevant only to π, leaving the residue Σ_L, which is mapped to λ. Σ itself is then mapped to π. The subsystem of C_{HL} mapping Σ to π is called the *PF component*; the subsystem of C_{HL} mapping Σ_L to λ is called the *LF component*; and the pre-Spell-Out system of C_{HL} is called the *overt syntax*.

An LI presented to a computation is taken to be a complex of three types of features. The LI *airplane*, for example, contains (a) phonological features such as [begins with vowel] that serve only to yield π, (b) semantic features such as [artifact] that serve only to yield λ, and (c) formal features such as [nominal] that enter into a computation but must be eliminated (at least by PF) for convergence. The collection of formal features FF[LI] of LI is then a subcomplex of LI accessible to C_{HL} (Chomsky 1995, 230).

A formal feature may or may not be strong. If it is strong, it must enter into a checking relation, forcing movement (or insertion). The [±strong] dimension is narrowly restricted by (1) (Chomsky 1995, 232).

(1) If F is strong, then F is a feature of a nonsubstantive category and F is checked by a categorial feature.

Given (1), nouns and main verbs do not bear strong features, and a strong feature forces movement (or insertion) of a certain category. To capture the timing of such forced movement (or insertion), Chomsky (1995, 234) proposes what we may call the *Strong Feature Condition* (SFC).

(2) *Strong Feature Condition*
Suppose that the derivation D has formed Σ containing α with a strong feature F. Then, D is canceled if α is in a category not headed by α.

Given (2), Chomsky (1995, 235) argues that the *Extended Projection Principle* (EPP) reduces to a strong D-feature of T, which is a categorial feature divorced from the Case feature of T. Suppose C_{HL} has formed structure (3), in which TP immediately dominates the head T (which bears a strong D-feature) and its complement VP.

(3)

Suppose, as a next step, C_{HL} concatenates TP and C, forming (4), in which CP immediately dominates the head C and its complement TP, whose head T still bears a strong D-feature.

(4)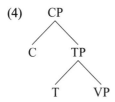

In (4), the head T with the strong D-feature is in the category not headed by T, namely, CP. Hence, this derivation (inducing a violation of the EPP) violates the SFC and cancels.[4]

A guiding idea of the Minimalist Program is that syntactic operations (e.g., subject raising) may apply anywhere without any special stipulation. If a wrong choice is made, C_{HL} must pay the penalty.

1.3   Bare Phrase Structure

C_{HL} can access LIs (minimal projections) and larger units (maximal projections) that are constructed from LIs (and those already formed). Given that bar levels are not inherent properties of lexical items, the minimal and maximal projections are entirely determined by the structure in which they appear: a category that does not project any further is a maximal projection XP, and one that is not a projection at all is a minimal projection X^{min}; any other is an X′ (invisible at the interface and for computation) (Chomsky 1994; 1995, 242–243).[5]

The simplest operation for constructing larger units from LIs (and those already formed) is *Merge* (Chomsky 1994; 1995, 243).

(5) *Merge*

   Applied to two objects α and β, Merge forms the new object K by concatenating α and β.

Merge applies to the two objects α and β. The output of this application is the new object K; α and β are eliminated.[6]

(6) Input: α, β

   ―――――――――――――――――――――

   Concatenate α and β, forming K

   ―――――――――――――――――――――

   Output: K

This application of Merge is illustrated in (7).

(7) a. α, β   b.

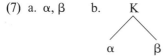

The simplest formulation of Merge applies at the root only (cyclic application).[7] The newly constructed object K is a set $\{\gamma, \{\alpha, \beta\}\}$, where α and β are constituents of K, and γ that identifies the type of K is a label of K. The label γ is further taken to be the head of either α or β. Suppose K is identified with the type of α. Then, $K = \{H(\alpha), \{\alpha, \beta\}\}$ where $H(\alpha)$ is the head of α, and K is a projection of $H(\alpha)$. K is represented informally as (8) (assuming no order), where the diagram is constructed from nodes paired with labels and pairs of such labeled nodes, and labels are distinguished by subscripts (Chomsky 1994; 1995, 244).

(8)

As shown in (8), the operation Merge that applies to two objects α and β is asymmetric, projecting either α or β. If α projects, then the head of α becomes the label of the newly formed object K. So, for example, Merge applies to two objects *the* and *book,* and forms a projection of *the*. The new object resulting from this application of Merge is {the, {the, book}}, informally represented as (9).

(9)

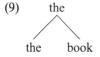

The functioning elements of {the, {the, book}} in a computation correspond to the nodes of the informal representation (9). They are called *terms* of {the, {the, book}} (Chomsky 1994; 1995, 247).

(10) a. K is a term of K.
     b. If L is a term of K, then the members of the members of L are terms of K.

Given (10), the terms of {the, {the, book}} are {the, {the, book}} itself, *the,* and *book.*

The concatenation operation can construct two distinct types of categories: a nonsegment category and a two-segment category (Chomsky 1986a; May 1985). To distinguish them, their labels are taken to be distinct: a nonsegment category projected from K in concatenating α and K is {H(K), {α, K}}; a two-segment category projected from K in concatenating α and K is {$\langle$H(K), H(K)$\rangle$, {α, K}} (Chomsky 1994; 1995, 248).

Merge forms the new object by concatenating two objects that are separate phrase markers. Forming a new object by concatenating two objects that are in a single phrase marker thus involves a second operation. This operation is called *Move* (Chomsky 1994; 1995, 250). Unlike Merge, Move is defined so as to operate at the root (cyclic application) as well as at the nonroot (noncyclic application).

(11) *Move*
     Applied to the category Σ with K and α, Move forms Σ' by concatenating α and K. This operation, if noncyclic, replaces K in Σ by L = {γ, {α, K}}.

Move applies to the object Σ. The output of this application is the new object Σ'; Σ is eliminated.[8] When applying at the root (cyclic application), Move functions just like Merge. Suppose C_{HL} has constructed the category Σ with a term α (i.e., $\Sigma = K$). Then, Move forms Σ' by concatenating α and Σ.

(12) Input: Σ (containing α)
     _____
     Concatenate α and Σ, forming Σ'
     _____
     Output: Σ'

This cyclic application of Move is illustrated in (13).

(13) a.

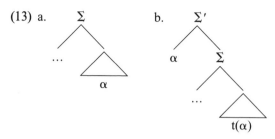

When applying at the nonroot (noncyclic application), Move performs a slightly more complex procedure. Suppose C_{HL} has constructed the category Σ with terms K and α (and say, K is a constituent of Σ). Then, Move concatenates α and K to form L and replaces K in Σ by L, forming Σ'.

(14) Input: Σ (containing K and α)

Concatenate α and K, forming $L = \{\gamma, \{\alpha, K\}\}$
Replace K in Σ by L, forming Σ'

Output: Σ'

This noncyclic application of Move is illustrated in (15).

(15) a.

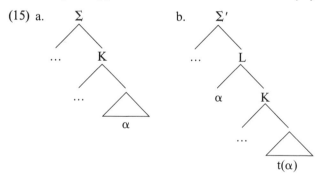

Like Merge, Move (incorporating the concatenation operation) can construct two distinct categories: a nonsegment category and a two-segment category. Unlike Merge (which operates on two separate phrase markers), Move (which operates on a single phrase marker) forms the chain CH (α, t(α)), where t(α) is a trace of α, or a complete copy of α under the copy theory of movement (Chomsky 1993).

In addition to the structure-building operations Merge and Move, C_{HL} incorporates a third operation, which performs an erasure process (making an element invisible) (Chomsky 1994; 1995, 250). A stronger form of such an operation is given in (16), which we may call *Erase* (Chomsky 1995, 280).

(16) *Erase*
    Applied to the category Σ with α containing F, Erase forms Σ′ by
    replacing F in α by the empty element ∅.

Erase applies to the object Σ. The output of this application is the new object Σ′; Σ is eliminated.[9] We take the empty element ∅ to be an actual symbol of mental representation with no feature. In the application of Erase, the empty element ∅ replaces F. That is, F is eliminated entirely: F is inaccessible to any operation, not just to interpretability at the interface(s). Suppose C_{HL} has constructed the category Σ with a term α containing F. Then, Erase replaces F in α by the empty element ∅, forming Σ′.

(17) Input: Σ (with α containing F)

Replace F in α by the empty element ∅, forming Σ′

Output: Σ′

This (noncyclic) application of Erase is illustrated in (18).

(18) a.   Σ   b.   Σ′

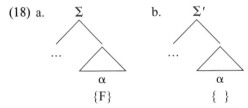

To summarize, under the bare phrase structure analysis incorporating Merge, Move, and Erase, the empirically desirable properties of the general X-bar-theoretic format are essentially deduced; minimal and maximal projections are relationally determined, and nonbranching projections are eliminated along with bar level features.[10,11]

1.4 Functional Categories

Postulation of a functional category has to be justified, either by output conditions (phonetic and/or semantic interpretation) or by theory-internal argument (Chomsky 1995, 240). The categories that concern us include T, D, C, Agr, and the light verb *v*.[12] The functional categories T, D, and C are arguably justified by their semantic interpretation: T bears a feature of [finiteness], D bears a feature of [referentiality], and C bears a [mood] feature (e.g., declarative, interrogative). But the functional categories Agr and the light verb *v* each have no interface interpretation, thereby calling for theory-internal arguments.

Within the Minimalist Program, postulation of the light verb *v* is justified as follows. Under the bare phrase structure analysis (incorporating the binary branching hypothesis), if a verb V has several internal arguments (e.g., *put*), it is necessary to postulate a "Larsonian shell" structure as in (19), where *v* is a light verb (requiring verbal affixation) to which V overtly adjoins.[13]

(19) a.   b.

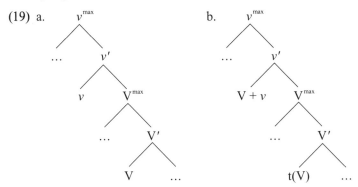

The internal arguments of V occupy the positions of specifier and complement of V, and the external argument of V occupies the specifier of *v*. Given this version of the predicate-internal subject hypothesis, the causative or agentive role of the external argument of V can be expressed by the *v*-V^{max} configuration.[14] Chomsky (1995, 315) extends this phrase structure analysis to transitive verb constructions as in (20): the internal argument Obj of a transitive verb V occupies the position inside V^{max}; the external argument Subj of V occupies the specifier of a light verb *v*; and V overtly adjoins to *v*.

(20) a.   b.

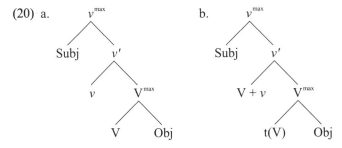

Given this extension, the basic structure of a clause containing a transitive verb is represented as (21) (prior to the adjunction of V to v).

(21)

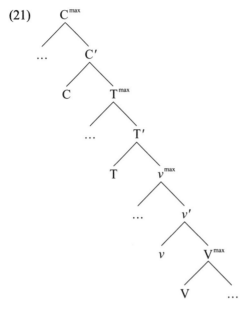

Adopting the structure (21), Chomsky (1995, sec. 4.10) argues that the position of an expletive in *multiple-subject constructions* (MSCs) is an additional (outer) specifier of T and the position of an overtly shifted object in languages such as Icelandic is an additional (outer) specifier of v. They are represented as (22a) and (22b), respectively.[15]

(22) a.   b.

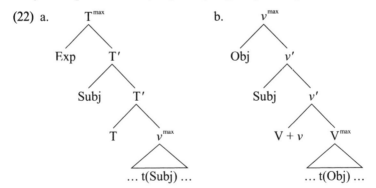

In (22a), insertion of an expletive Exp follows raising of a subject Subj for checking of the strong D-feature of T. In (22b), the v-V^{max} configuration assigns the role of the external argument of V to the inner specifier position of v; hence, the shifting of an object Obj must follow the concatenation of Subj and a projection of v.[16,17] Although postulation of the light verb v is justified by the theory-internal argument presented above, postulation of the functional category Agr receives no such support. Following Chomsky (1995), I develop minimalist analyses that dispense with the functional category Agr.

1.5 Checking Theory

The force driving syntactic operations such as Move is morphological necessity: some feature F must be checked. If so, minimalist assumptions suggest that C_{HL} raises only the feature F to satisfy this feature-checking requirement. Following this guiding intuition, Move α is replaced by the more principled operation Move F, F a feature. This modification extends the class of syntactic objects to include $K = \{H(\alpha), \{F, \alpha\}\}$ (Chomsky 1995, 262).

In the overt syntax, however, Move F raises more than the feature F, suggesting that the raising of the larger unit containing F is required by the interface conditions. Chomsky (1995, 262) proposes that Move raises the feature F along with just enough material necessary for convergence. He argues that in the overt syntax, Move raises α, where α is the smallest category containing the feature F that allows convergence: a kind of generalized pied-piping. In the overt syntax, α is taken to be a category, given that isolated features and other scattered parts of words induce a violation of the interface conditions imposed by the A-P system: they are simply unpronounceable. In the LF component, however, being free from the A-P interface conditions, Move raises a minimal unit containing the feature F. Such a minimal unit containing F is understood to be FF[F].

Assuming this feature movement analysis, the checking configuration of features is defined as follows (Chomsky 1995, 299). First, assume all notions to be irreflexive unless otherwise indicated. Given the standard notion of *domination* for the pair (δ, β), δ a segment, the category K *includes* β if every segment of K dominates β, and the category K *contains* β if some segment of K dominates β. Now suppose α is an X^0 category (or a feature), and CH is a trivial chain α as in (23a) or a nontrivial chain $(\alpha, t(\alpha))$ as in (23b).

(23) a.

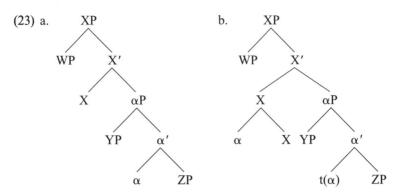

Max(α) is defined as the smallest maximal projection including α. Thus, Max(α) in (23a) is αP, whereas Max(α) in (23b) is XP. The *domain* δ(CH) of CH is the set of categories included in Max(α) that are distinct from and do not contain α or t(α).[18] Thus, the δ(CH) in (23a) is the set of YP, ZP, and whatever these categories dominate, whereas δ(CH) in (23b) is the set of WP, YP, ZP, and whatever these categories dominate. The *complement domain* of CH is the subset of δ(CH) reflexively dominated by the complement of the construction. Thus, the complement domain of CH in (23a) is the set of ZP and whatever it dominates, whereas the complement domain of CH in (23b) is the set of YP, ZP, and whatever these categories dominate. The remainder of δ(CH) is the *residue* of CH. Thus, the residue of CH in (23a) is its domain minus ZP and whatever it dominates, whereas the residue of CH in (23b) is its domain minus YP, ZP, and whatever they dominate. The *minimal domain* Min(δ(CH)) of CH is the smallest subset K of δ(CH) such that for any γ ∈ δ(CH), some β ∈ K reflexively dominates γ. Thus, Min(δ(CH)) in (23a) is {YP, ZP}, whereas Min(δ(CH)) in (23b) is {WP, YP, ZP}. The minimal complement domain of CH is the *internal domain* of CH. Thus, the internal domain of CH in (23a) is {ZP}, whereas the internal domain of CH in (23b) is {YP, ZP}. Finally, the minimal residue of CH is the *checking domain* of CH, where a feature can enter into a checking relation with CH (the checking configuration). Thus, the checking domain of CH in (23a) is {YP}, whereas the checking domain of CH in (23b) is {WP}. Note that domain and minimal domain are understood derivationally, not representationally: they are defined "once and for all" for each CH.

Suppose that features match in the checking configuration. Then they are checked automatically, and erased immediately *when possible*, where possibility is to be understood relative to other principles. Specifically, a checked feature cannot be erased if that operation would violate the overriding principle of recoverability. That is, certain features, which may be called [+interpretable], enter into interpretation at the interface; others, which may be called [−interpretable], are uninterpretable and must be eliminated for convergence (Chomsky 1995, 277). Given this crucial distinction, a checked [+interpretable] feature cannot be erased and hence continues to be accessible to C_{HL} even after it is checked; a checked [−interpretable] feature will be erased immediately and hence becomes inaccessible to C_{HL} (Chomsky 1995, 280). For example, [+interpretable] features such as ϕ-features of nouns are accessible to C_{HL} throughout, whether checked or not, whereas [−interpretable] features such as Case features of nouns are inaccessible to C_{HL} once checked and erased.[19,20]

1.6 Computational Principles

The Minimalist Program, seeking a maximally simple design for language, presumes that such a design reduces the degree of *computational complexity*. One way to reduce such complexity is to postulate principles that constrain syntactic operations (in particular, the operation Move), which we may call *computational principles*. Chomsky (1995, 297) proposes that formulation of such computational principles (which restrict the class of legitimate applications of Move) is more natural if the movement of α to enter into a checking relation with β is interpreted as β *attracting* α, instead of α *moving to* β. Given this proposal, let us examine the computational principles (formulated as such).

The c-command relation between the head and the tail of the chain can be captured by the *C-Command Condition*, a computational principle (adapted from Chomsky 1995, 253).

(24) *C-Command Condition*
     H(K) attracts α only if H(K) c-commands α.

We adopt the standard definition of *c-command* (Reinhart 1976).[21]

(25) α c-commands β iff every category dominating α dominates β,
     α ≠ β, and neither dominates the other.

The C-Command Condition ensures that H(K) cannot attract any category outside its c-command domain. Following Chomsky (1995, 297), let us further assume (26).

(26) Move concatenates α and K if H(K) attracts α.

Given (26), the C-Command Condition prohibits Move from moving α downward or sideways: movement of α is necessarily upward (in the specific sense defined by c-command). Note that unlike Chomsky (1995), we take the head H(K) of the target K (rather than the target K itself) to be the category attracting α.[22]

The principle *Last Resort* (LR) is also formulated as a computational principle (Chomsky 1995, 280).

(27) *Last Resort*

H(K) attracts α only if α enters into a checking relation with a sublabel of K, where a sublabel of K is a feature of the zero-level projection $H(K)^{0max}$ (including those features adjoined to H(K)).

LR ensures that H(K) attracts α only if some features of α and $H(K)^{0max}$ (including those features adjoined to H(K)) match. If there are no such features, given (26), LR prohibits Move from concatenating α and K. The morphologically driven property of Move is therefore captured.[23]

Deviant examples such as (28) require a further restriction on C_{HL} (Lasnik and Saito 1992; Rizzi 1990).

(28) *$[_{TP}[_\alpha$ John] seems [that $[_\beta$ it] was told t(α) $[_{CP}$ that ...]]]

In (28), neither the C-Command Condition nor LR is violated. The matrix T c-commands α (satisfying the C-Command Condition) and α can enter into a checking relation with the matrix T (satisfying LR). Hence, nothing prevents the matrix T from attracting α. Thus, contrary to fact, we expect that Move should be able to concatenate α and the matrix TP, forming (28). To exclude this application of Move, the *Minimal Link Condition* (MLC) is incorporated into the system (Chomsky 1995, 311).[24]

(29) *Minimal Link Condition*

H(K) attracts α only if there is no β, β closer to H(K) than α, such that H(K) attracts β.

The notion "closer" has been interpreted in terms of *c-command* and *equidistance* (Chomsky 1993, 1994). Under the attraction theory of movement, the principle of *equidistance* is formulated as (30) (Chomsky 1995, 299).

(30) β does not prevent H(K) from attracting α if β is in the minimal domain of CH, where CH is the chain headed by γ, and γ is adjoined to H(K).

The notion "closer," now understood in terms of c-command (25) and equidistance (30), is defined as (31) (Chomsky 1995, 299).[25]

(31) β is closer to H(K) than α iff β c-commands α, and β is not in the minimal domain of CH, where CH is the chain headed by γ, and γ is adjoined to H(K).

Given (31), the MLC excludes the derivation of (28) as follows. In the derivation of (28), prior to the raising of α to the specifier of the matrix T, α is c-commanded by β, and β is not in the minimal domain of CH the head of which is adjoined to the matrix T. Hence, β is closer to the matrix T than α. In addition, β is c-commanded by the matrix T, and β can enter into a checking relation with the matrix T (e.g., β and the matrix T match in terms of D-feature). Thus, the MLC prohibits the matrix T from attracting α: Move cannot concatenate α and TP. The shortest movement property of Move is therefore captured.

Incorporation of the principle of equidistance into the definition of closeness is motivated by examples such as (32) (drawn from Icelandic), in which overt subject raising crosses over the shifted object, yielding a seemingly problematic crossing path (see, among others, Holmberg 1986; Jonas and Bobaljik 1993; Thráinsson 1993).

(32) Risarnir   átu₁ ríkisstjórnia₂   [$_{vP}$ ekki t₁ t₂].
     the-giants ate the-government   not
     'The giants did not eat the government.'

Let us examine the relevant aspects of the derivation of (32).[26] At some point in the derivation, C_{HL} constructs (33).[27]

(33)
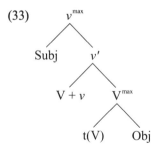

The next step must fill the outer specifier of v (to which V is already adjoined). Given that v does not c-command Subj, the C-Command Condition prohibits v from attracting Subj. The only category that v can attract is Obj. Therefore, C_{HL} concatenates Obj and v^{max}, forming (34).

(34)

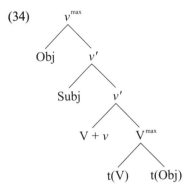

At a later stage in the derivation, C_{HL} reaches (35).

(35)

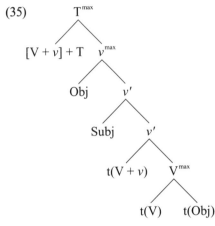

The next step must fill the specifier of T (to which the complex head V + v is already adjoined), in order to check the strong D-feature of T (see section 1.2). If the notion "closer" were defined solely in terms of c-command, Obj (which c-commands Subj) would be closer to T than Subj. Consequently, the MLC would prohibit T from attracting Subj. The principle of equidistance must therefore be incorporated into the definition of closeness. Given the notion "closer" defined in terms of c-command and equidistance, Obj, intervening between T and Subj, does not prevent T from attracting Subj. T can attract Subj because Obj is in the minimal domain of CH (V + v, t(V + v)) the head of which is adjoined to T. Thus, C_{HL} concatenates Subj and T^{max}, forming (36).[28]

(36)

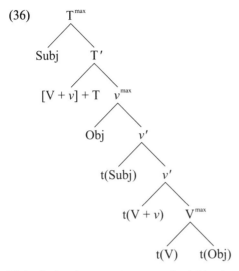

This derivation continues and yields the legitimate interface representations of (32), as desired.

To summarize, given the computational principles of UG—namely, the C-Command Condition, LR, and the MLC—the class of legitimate applications of Move is restricted and the degree of computational complexity is reduced. Under the attraction theory of movement, deviant examples such as (28) (in which neither the C-Command Condition nor LR is violated) are excluded by the MLC. Incorporation of the principle of equidistance into the definition of closeness is motivated by examples such as (32) (in which C_{HL} forms a seemingly problematic crossing path, with the Subj crossing over the shifted Obj).

I will continue to refer to the operation of movement as *Move*, though assuming that its correct interpretation is in terms of *attraction*.

1.7   Economy Principles

The economy principles apply to both representations and derivations (Chomsky 1991, 1993, 1994, 1995).

Economy of representation is nothing other than the condition of *Full Interpretation* (FI): every object at the interface must receive an "external" interpretation. In order to be interpreted by the A-P system and the C-I system, each representation must consist of legitimate objects at the interface. PF is a representation in universal phonetics, with no indication of syntactic or morphological features. At LF, each legitimate object is taken to be a chain CH $(\alpha_1, \ldots, \alpha_n)$ (at least a head chain, an argument chain, a modifier chain, or an operator-variable chair).[29] We say that a derivation D yielding a pair (π, λ) converges if π and λ satisfy FI at PF and at LF, respectively; otherwise, D crashes. Thus, FI is a convergence condition, meaning that FI determines the set of convergent derivations.

Economy of derivation, on the other hand, determines whether a convergent derivation D from a numeration N to a pair (π, λ) is optimal: the economy principles hold only among convergent derivations and determine the set of optimal convergent derivations.[30]

In light of derivational economy, crosslinguistic variation concerning the timing of verb movement is captured as follows. In languages such as English, a convergent derivation involving covert verb movement is more economical than its competing convergent derivation(s) involving overt verb movement. *Procrastinate* is a principle of derivational economy, incorporated into the system to capture the postponement of such *unforced* overt operations until the LF component.[31]

(37) *Procrastinate*
    Minimize the number of overt operations necessary for convergence.

In English, overt verb movement is not required for convergence; hence, Procrastinate forces verb movement to be covert. In languages such as French, however, Procrastinate permits verb movement to be overt, given that overt verb movement (for the checking of the strong V-feature of T in French) is required for convergence.[32]

In pursuing the economy approach, another principle of derivational economy is necessary to block the following unwanted convergent derivation with no violation of Procrastinate. In languages such as Icelandic, Subj must undergo overt subject raising, whereas Obj may undergo overt object shift: T requires one specifier and the light verb v permits two specifiers (see the discussion below (32)). Suppose Obj overtly shifts to the outer specifier of v, then further raises to the specifier of T. Then, the relevant features (including the D-feature of T) are checked. But notice that Subj in the inner specifier of v and T still bear unchecked [−interpretable] features, namely, Case features; consequently, FF[Subj] covertly adjoins to T. This derivation induces no violation of Procrastinate and converges, exhibiting the O-V-S order, contrary to fact. To block this unwanted but still convergent derivation, the *Shortest Derivation Condition* (SDC) is incorporated into the system.[33]

(38) *Shortest Derivation Condition*
   Minimize the number of operations necessary for convergence.

Recall that the unwanted convergent derivation above involves three applications of Move: (a) overt object shift to the outer specifier of v, (b) overt object raising to the specifier of T, and (c) covert FF[Subj] raising to T. However, only two applications of Move would suffice for convergence: (a) overt object shift to the outer specifier of v and (b) overt subject raising to the specifier of T. Therefore, the SDC blocks the former unwanted convergent derivation in favor of the latter convergent derivation with *one application fewer* (Chomsky 1995, 357).

   In the following chapter, assuming the central aspects of the Minimalist Program reviewed here, I examine in detail the functions of syntactic operations (e.g., Merge, Move, and Erase) and the formulation of the SDC.

Chapter 2

Shortest Derivation and Timing Effects

A central question that I address in this chapter is, What counts as an operation in the eyes of derivational economy, in particular the Shortest Derivation Condition (SDC)? I provide an answer to this question that requires a minimal modification of the SDC. As an immediate consequence of this modification, the empirically desirable aspects of *strict cyclicity* are shown to be deducible. As a natural extension of this modification, the timing effects motivating Procrastinate are also shown to be explicable.

2.1 Elementary Operations: A Proposal

Under minimalist assumptions, C_{HL} selects LIs from a numeration N and performs a structure-building procedure to form a pair (π, λ). The structure-building operations of C_{HL} are Merge, Move, and Erase. In this section, I examine the two distinct but closely related operations Merge and Move, and I show them to be unifiable in terms of elementary operations (to be made precise below). The seemingly unrelated operation Erase will be discussed in section 2.3.

First recall the definition of Merge, repeated in (1).

(1) *Merge*
    Applied to two objects α and β, Merge forms the new object K by concatenating α and β.

Merge is defined so as to operate on two separate phrase markers and apply at the root only (cyclic application).[1] The output of this application is K (i.e., K is substituted for (α, β)).

(2) Input: α, β

_____

Concatenate α and β, forming K

_____

Output: K

This cyclic application of Merge, involving the elementary operation of concatenation, is illustrated in (3).

(3) a. α, β   b.   K

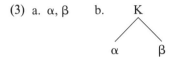

Merge employs the elementary operation of concatenation only, and it cannot apply at the nonroot (noncyclic application). However, we can of course revise the definition of Merge as (4), in which the elementary operation of replacement is incorporated, so that both cyclic and noncyclic applications are permitted.

(4) *Merge*
    Applied to two objects α and Σ with β, Merge forms Σ′ by
    concatenating α and β. This operation, if noncyclic, replaces β in Σ
    by $L = \{\gamma, \{\alpha, \beta\}\}$.

Merge given in (4) (Merge (4)), unlike Merge given in (1) (Merge (1)), employs the elementary operations of both concatenation and replacement, and it can apply at the root (cyclic application) or nonroot (noncyclic application). The output of this application is Σ′ (i.e., Σ′ is substituted for (α, Σ)). When applying at the root (i.e., β = Σ), Merge (4) functions just like Merge (1). Suppose C_{HL} has selected the two objects α and Σ. Then, Merge (4) forms the new object Σ′ by concatenating α and Σ.

(5) Input: α, Σ

_____

Concatenate α and Σ, forming Σ′

_____

Output: Σ′

This cyclic application of Merge (4), involving the elementary operation of concatenation, is illustrated in (6).

(6) a. α, Σ   b.   Σ′

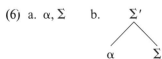

When applying at the nonroot (i.e., $\beta \neq \Sigma$), Merge (4) performs a slightly more complex procedure. Suppose C_{HL} has constructed the object Σ with a term β (and say, β is a constituent of Σ) and has selected the object α. Then, Merge (4) performs the following two steps: (a) to concatenate α and β, forming L, and (b) to replace β in Σ by L, forming Σ'.

(7) Input: α, Σ (containing β)

Concatenate α and β, forming $L = \{\gamma, \{\alpha, \beta\}\}$
Replace β in Σ by L, forming Σ'

Output: Σ'

This noncyclic application of Merge (4), involving the elementary operations of both concatenation and replacement, is illustrated in (8).[2]

(8) a. α, Σ b. Σ'

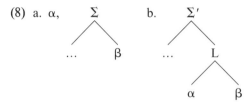

What this application of Merge (4) does is to embed α within some construction Σ already formed.

Chomsky (1995, 248) argues that any additional complication in the formulation of Merge would require strong empirical motivation. Given no such empirical motivation, he suggests that Merge should be defined in the simplest form, namely, Merge (1). Since both Merge (1) and Merge (4) employ an elementary operation of concatenation, the additional complication of Merge (4) comes down to an additional elementary operation of replacement. I will come back to this point shortly.

The situation is quite different for Move. Move is defined in terms of concatenation and replacement. Its definition is repeated in (9).

(9) *Move*
   Applied to the category Σ with K and α, Move forms Σ' by
   concatenating α and K. This operation, if noncyclic, replaces K in
   Σ by $L = \{\gamma, \{\alpha, K\}\}$.

Move is defined so as to operate on a single phrase marker and to apply at the root (cyclic application) or nonroot (noncyclic application). The output of this application is Σ' (i.e., Σ' is substituted for Σ). When applying at the root (i.e., $K = \Sigma$), Move functions as follows. Suppose C_{HL} has constructed the category Σ with a term α. Then, Move forms Σ′ by concatenating α and Σ.

(10) Input: Σ (containing α)

────────────────────────────────

Concatenate α and Σ, forming Σ′

────────────────────────────────

Output: Σ′

This cyclic application of Move, involving the elementary operation of concatenation, is illustrated in (11).

(11) a.   Σ   b.   Σ′

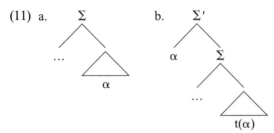

When applying at the nonroot (i.e., K ≠ Σ), Move performs a slightly more complex procedure, just like Merge (4). Suppose C_{HL} has constructed the category Σ with terms K and α (and say, K is a constituent of Σ). Then, Move performs the following two steps: (a) to concatenate α and K, forming L, and (b) to replace K in Σ by L, forming Σ′.

(12) Input: Σ (containing K and α)

───

Concatenate α and K, forming L = {γ, {α, K}}
Replace K in Σ by L, forming Σ′

───

Output: Σ′

This noncyclic application of Move, involving the elementary operations of both concatenation and replacement, is illustrated in (13).[3,4]

(13) a.   Σ   b.   Σ′

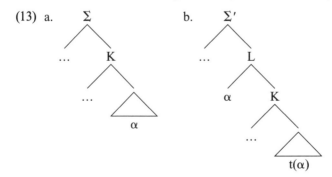

Unlike noncyclic application of Merge (4), noncyclic application of Move is motivated on independent grounds (e.g., head movement is an instance of noncyclic application of Move). Thus, the definition of Move given in (9) is justified.

Under the system developed in Chomsky 1995, the "complex" formulation of Merge (given in (4)) is banned since empirically unmotivated. Thus, the "strict cyclicity" property of merger is ensured by definition. By contrast, the "complex" formulation of Move (given in (9)) is permitted since empirically justified. But notice that this analysis does not explain the "strict cyclicity" property of overt movement—that is, why C_{HL} necessarily selects cyclic application of Move (which performs a "simple" procedure involving the elementary operation of concatenation only) over noncyclic application of Move (which performs a "complex" procedure involving the elementary operations of both concatenation and replacement) if both applications allow convergence (see, among others, Chomsky 1993; Kitahara 1994a, 1995).

To provide a principled and unified account of the preference for a "simple" procedure over a "complex" one in syntactic application (i.e., the "strict cyclicity" properties of merger and overt movement), I first adopt the "complex" formulation of Merge (4) (henceforth, Merge), thereby allowing Merge to apply at the root (cyclic application) or non-root (noncyclic application). Given this, Merge and Move perform a "simple" procedure involving the elementary operation of concatenation when they apply cyclically, whereas they perform a "complex" procedure involving the elementary operations of both concatenation and replacement when they apply noncyclically. Now recall that what makes the "complex" procedure *complex* is that it employs the additional elementary operation of replacement. Under the proposed analysis, the simple (cyclic) procedure is characterized as the elementary operation of concatenation only, whereas the complex (noncyclic) procedure is characterized as the elementary operations of both concatenation and replacement. Given this characterization of *complexity*, I am ready to provide a principled answer to the question, What determines the choice between the simple (cyclic) procedure and the complex (noncyclic) procedure?

I propose that such a choice is determined by derivational economy. Specifically, I revise the Shortest Derivation Condition (SDC), "Minimize the number of operations necessary for convergence" (Chomsky 1991, 1993; Epstein 1992), as "Minimize the number of the *elementary* operations (i.e., concatenation and replacement) necessary for convergence."[5]

(14) *Shortest Derivation Condition (revised)*
Minimize the number of elementary operations necessary for convergence.

Although C_{HL} can, in principle, perform cyclic and noncyclic applications of Merge and Move (see (15a–d)), the SDC makes sure that C_{HL} minimizes the number of elementary operations necessary for convergence.

(15) a. cyclic application of Merge (= concatenation)
b. cyclic application of Move (= concatenation)
c. noncyclic application of Merge (= concatenation + replacement)
d. noncyclic application of Move (= concatenation + replacement)

Notice that the choice between cyclic and noncyclic applications of Merge does not affect convergence; hence, C_{HL} must select cyclic application of Merge employing only one elementary operation over noncyclic application of Merge employing two elementary operations. That is, the SDC determines the choice between cyclic and noncyclic applications of Merge and ensures the "strict cyclicity" property of merger.

In the following two sections, I examine various cases involving the choices among (15a–d). In section 2.2, I demonstrate that the "strict cyclicity" property of overt movement is also captured by the SDC. In section 2.3, I examine the operation Erase, in particular its relation to the timing of the application of Move, and I argue that the empirically desirable aspects of Procrastinate are also deducible from the SDC.

2.2 Strict Cyclicity: Past and Present

In this section, I first review three previous minimalist analyses of island violation phenomena with particular attention to *strict cyclicity* (Chomsky 1993, 1994, 1995).[6,7] I then demonstrate that the Shortest Derivation Condition (SDC), which requires that the number of elementary operations necessary for convergence be minimized, captures the "strict cyclicity" property of overt movement: overt cyclic application of Move blocks overt noncyclic application of Move if both applications allow convergence.

2.2.1 An Extension Condition Analysis
Chomsky (1993) eliminates D-Structure as a level of representation.[8] He then (re)introduces the single structure-building operation *Generalized Transformation* (GT) (Chomsky 1955).

(16) *Generalized Transformation*
   GT targets a category α, adds an empty element $\emptyset$ external to α, takes a category β, and substitutes β for $\emptyset$, forming the new phrase structure γ, which satisfies X-bar theory.

GT constructs a single phrase structure (using categories selected from the lexicon as well as categories already constructed by GT), in accordance with the *Extension Condition* (EC).

(17) *Extension Condition*
   GT must extend the entire phrase structure (containing the target of GT).

Intuitively, the EC asserts that GT must build the entire phrase structure *bigger*: GT must create a dominator of its input tree.[9] In addition to the EC, the *Shortest Movement Condition* (SMC) is incorporated into the system.

(18) *Shortest Movement Condition*
   Given two convergent derivations D_1 and D_2, both minimal and containing the same number of steps, D_1 blocks D_2 if its links are shorter.

Chomsky (1993, 15) explains that the SMC prohibits any derivation in which a category has skipped a position it could have reached by a shorter move, had that position not been filled. Let us see exactly how Chomsky's (1993) system captures the deviance of island violation phenomena such as the *wh*-island violation (19).

(19) *How$_2$ did John wonder [what$_1$ Mary fixed t_1 t_2]?

First consider the relevant aspects of the noncyclic derivation of (19), given in (20).

(20) a. [$_{CP}$ how [$_{C'}$ C$_{wh}$ [$_{IP}$ John wondered
      [$_{CP}$ C$_{wh}$ [$_{IP}$ Mary fixed what t(how)]]]]]]
   b. [$_{CP}$ how [$_{C'}$ C$_{wh}$ [$_{IP}$ John wondered
      [$_{CP}$ what [$_{C'}$ C$_{wh}$ [$_{IP}$ Mary fixed t(what) t(how)]]]]]]]

In (20a), GT raising *how* to the matrix CP satisfies the EC and the SMC (given that the specifier of the embedded CP was not projected at this point in the derivation). In (20b), GT raising *what* to the embedded CP satisfies the SMC, but it violates the EC because this noncyclic application of GT fails to extend the entire phrase structure, namely, the matrix

CP. Now consider the relevant aspects of the cyclic derivation of (19), given in (21).

(21) a. [CP what [C′ Cwh [IP Mary fixed t(what) how]]]
     b. [CP how [C′ Cwh [IP John wondered
        [CP what [C′ Cwh [IP Mary fixed t(what) t(how)]]]]]]

In (21a), GT raising *what* to the nearest CP satisfies the EC and the SMC. In (21b), GT raising *how* to the matrix CP satisfies the EC, but it violates the SMC because *how* has skipped a position it could have reached by a shorter move, had that position not been filled, namely, the specifier of the embedded C. Under Chomsky's (1993) system, therefore, the EC excludes the noncyclic derivation of (19), whereas the SMC excludes the cyclic derivation of (19).

2.2.2 A Minimal Link Condition Analysis

Chomsky (1994) proposes a number of new analyses, one of which offers a different account of the deviant (19). Chomsky first replaces GT by two structure-building operations Merge and Move, repeated here.[10]

(22) *Merge*
     Applied to two objects α and β, Merge forms the new object K by concatenating α and β.

(23) *Move*
     Applied to the category Σ with K and α, Move forms Σ' by concatenating α with K. This operation, if noncyclic, replaces K in Σ by $L = \{\gamma, \{\alpha, K\}\}$.

Concerning the "shortest movement" property of Move, Chomsky replaces the SMC by the following intuitive idea of the *Minimal Link Condition* (MLC).

(24) *Minimal Link Condition*
     Minimize chain links.

Chomsky (1994, 42) interprets (24) to mean that Move α must attach α to the nearest target in the already formed structure in a way that does not cause the derivation to crash. Given this interpretation, he argues that the MLC excludes both noncyclic and cyclic derivations of (19), thereby making it possible to eliminate the EC. Let us see exactly how Chomsky's (1994) system excludes these two derivations of (19).

First consider the relevant aspects of the noncyclic derivation of (19), given in (20). In (20a), Move raising *how* to the matrix CP violates the MLC given that its nearest target is the embedded CP (with no specifier), whereas in (20b), Move raising *what* to the embedded CP satisfies the MLC. Now consider the relevant aspects of the cyclic derivation of (19), given in (21). In (21a), Move raising *what* to the nearest CP satisfies the MLC, whereas in (21b), Move raising *how* to the matrix CP violates the MLC, given that its nearest target is the embedded CP (with a specifier, namely, *what*). Under Chomsky's (1994) system, therefore, the MLC excludes both noncyclic and cyclic derivations of (19), and it does so without any reference to the EC.

However, the MLC analysis, unlike the EC analysis, permits certain noncyclic derivations. Consider the subject island violation (25).

(25) ??Who$_2$ did you say that [pictures of t$_2$]$_1$ were stolen t$_1$?

The relevant aspects of the noncyclic and cyclic derivations of (25) are as follows.

(26) a. [$_{CP}$ who [$_{C'}$ C$_{wh}$ [$_{IP}$ you said
       [$_{CP}$ that [$_{IP}$ were stolen [$_\alpha$ pictures of t(who)]]]]]]
   b. [$_{CP}$ who [$_{C'}$ C$_{wh}$ [$_{IP}$ you said
       [$_{CP}$ that [$_{IP}$[$_\alpha$ pictures of t(who)] were stolen t(α)]]]]]

(27) a. [$_{IP}$[$_\alpha$ pictures of who] were stolen t(α)]
   b. [$_{CP}$ who [$_{C'}$ C$_{wh}$ [$_{IP}$ you said
       [$_{CP}$ that [$_{IP}$[$_\alpha$ pictures of t(who)] were stolen t(α)]]]]]

In the relevant aspects of the noncyclic derivation of (25), given in (26), the extraction of *who* out of α precedes the raising of α to the embedded subject position; hence, *who* is extracted out of α in the embedded object position. In the relevant aspects of the cyclic derivation of (25), given in (27), the raising of α to the embedded subject position precedes the extraction of *who* out of α; hence, *who* is extracted out of α in the embedded subject position. Given this, the *Subject Condition*, stated in (28), is violated only in the cyclic derivation of (25) (see, among others, Chomsky 1973).[11,12]

(28) *Subject Condition*
    Extraction out of a subject is prohibited.

Whereas the EC analysis excludes the noncyclic derivation of (25), which could have circumvented a violation of the Subject Condition, the MLC analysis fails to exclude it because no application of Move in the non-cyclic derivation of (25) (see (26a–b)) induces a violation of the MLC, given that the nearest target for Move raising *who* is the matrix CP and the nearest target for Move raising α is the embedded IP.

To summarize, Chomsky's (1993) analysis of the deviant (19) and (25) crucially relies on the EC to force the cyclic derivations of (19) and (25) (see (21), (27)), which violate the SMC and the Subject Condition, respectively. Chomsky's (1994) analysis of the deviant (19) crucially relies on the interpretation of the MLC to exclude the noncyclic and cyclic derivations of (19) (see (20), (21)). As for the deviant (25), Chomsky must appeal to a proper theory of economy of derivation that, he speculates, forces the cyclic derivation of (25), which violates the Subject Condition (see (27)).[13]

2.2.3   A Strong Feature Condition Analysis

Chomsky (1995) advances the Minimalist Program with several new proposals, one of which concerns feature strength. Chomsky (1995, 234) takes a descriptive property of strong features to be what we may call the *Strong Feature Condition* (SFC).

(29) *Strong Feature Condition*
     Suppose that the derivation D has formed Σ containing α with a strong feature F. Then, D is canceled if α is in a category not headed by α.

He then shows that the empirically desirable aspects of strict cyclicity follow naturally from the SFC. Consider the following steps of the non-cyclic derivation of (19) and the noncyclic derivation of (25), given in (30) and (31), respectively:

(30) a. [$_{CP}$ C_{wh} [$_{IP}$ Mary fixed what how]]
     b. [$_{VP}$ wondered [$_{CP}$ C_{wh} [$_{IP}$ Mary fixed what how]]]

(31) a. [$_{TP}$ were stolen [$_{\alpha}$ pictures of who]]
     b. [$_{CP}$ that [$_{TP}$ were stolen [$_{\alpha}$ pictures of who]]]

In mapping (30a) to (30b), Merge forms the matrix VP by concatenating the verb *wondered* and the CP the head of which still bears the strong *wh*-feature (taken to be a variant of D (Chomsky 1995, 289)). As a result of this application, the head C with the strong feature is in the matrix VP, a category not headed by the C; the noncyclic derivation of (19) is canceled at this point in the derivation. The same analysis holds for the application of Merge in (31). In mapping (31a) to (31b), Merge forms the CP by concatenating the complementizer *that* and the TP the head of which still bears the strong D-feature. As a result of this application, the head T with the strong feature is in the CP, a category not headed by the T; the non-cyclic derivation of (25) is canceled at this point in the derivation. As shown above, the "strict cyclicity" property of overt movement follows naturally from the descriptive property of strong features incorporated in the SFC.

To exclude the cyclic derivation of (19), Chomsky (1995) appeals to the more elaborated version of the *Minimal Link Condition* (MLC), given in (32).

(32) *Minimal Link Condition*
H(K) attracts α only if there is no β, β closer to H(K) than α, such that H(K) attracts β.

The notion "closer" is defined as (33).

(33) β is closer to H(K) than α iff β c-commands α, and β is not in the minimal domain of CH, where CH is the chain headed by γ, and γ is adjoined to H(K).

In the cyclic derivation of (19), the MLC prohibits Move from concatenating *how* and the matrix CP. Consider the following mapping:

(34) a. [$_{CP}$ C$_{wh}$ [$_{IP}$ John wondered
    [$_{CP}$ what [$_{C'}$ C$_{wh}$ [$_{IP}$ Mary fixed t(what) how]]]]]
 b. [$_{CP}$ how [$_{C'}$ C$_{wh}$ [$_{IP}$ John wondered
    [$_{CP}$ what [$_{C'}$ C$_{wh}$ [$_{IP}$ Mary fixed t(what) t(how)]]]]]]

In mapping (34a) to (34b), Move concatenates *how* and the matrix CP and checks the strong *wh*-feature of the matrix C. This application of Move violates the MLC, given that *what* in the specifier of the embedded C is closer to the matrix C than *how*, and that *what* can check the strong *wh*-feature of the matrix C.

Finally, to exclude the cyclic derivation of (25), the SFC analysis, like its rival analyses, appeals to the Subject Condition.

To summarize, under Chomsky's (1995) system, the SFC excludes the noncyclic derivations of (19) and (25) (see (20), (26)), the MLC excludes the cyclic derivation of (19) (see (21)), and the Subject Condition excludes the cyclic derivation of (25) (see (27)).

2.2.4 A Shortest Derivation Condition Analysis

The SFC captures the "strict cyclicity" property of overt movement without special stipulation, but the formulation of the SFC given in (29) itself remains highly descriptive.

Suppose we reformulate the SFC to be part of the definition of Spell-Out as follows:

(35) *Strong Feature Condition (revised)*
      Spell-Out applies to Σ only if Σ contains no category with a strong feature.

The SFC given in (35) is simpler, hence is to be preferred if tenable. Now notice that, under this simpler formulation, the strong feature of α can be checked any time before Spell-Out applies to the root containing α; hence, the "strict cyclicity" property of overt movement no longer follows from the property of feature strength.

In this subsection, assuming that neither a violation of the MLC nor a violation of the Subject Condition necessarily causes the derivation to crash, I demonstrate that the Shortest Derivation Condition (SDC), motivated on independent grounds, captures the "strict cyclicity" property of overt movement. Thus, the simpler formulation of the SFC (given in (35)) is compatible with the conclusion drawn from Chomsky 1995, namely, that strict cyclicity need not be specially stipulated (see chapter 4 for further elaboration). The SDC is repeated in (36).

(36) *Shortest Derivation Condition*
      Minimize the number of elementary operations necessary for convergence.

Under the SDC analysis, we expect that the noncyclic derivations of (19) and (25) are blocked by their more economical competitors. I argue that such competitors are, in fact, the cyclic derivations of (19) and (25).

First consider the deviant (19) and the relevant aspects of its noncyclic and cyclic derivations, given in (20) and (21), repeated here.

(19) *How$_2$ did John wonder [what$_1$ Mary fixed t$_1$ t$_2$]?

(20) a. [$_{CP}$ how [$_{C'}$ C_{wh} [$_{IP}$ John wondered
          [$_{CP}$ C_{wh} [$_{IP}$ Mary fixed what t(how)]]]]]
      b. [$_{CP}$ how [$_{C'}$ C_{wh} [$_{IP}$ John wondered
          [$_{CP}$ what [$_{C'}$ C_{wh} [$_{IP}$ Mary fixed t(what) t(how)]]]]]]

(21) a. $[_{CP}$ what $[_{C'}$ C_{wh} $[_{IP}$ Mary fixed t(what) how]]]

    b. $[_{CP}$ how $[_{C'}$ C_{wh} $[_{IP}$ John wondered

       $[_{CP}$ what $[_{C'}$ C_{wh} $[_{IP}$ Mary fixed t(what) t(how)]]]]]]

The noncyclic derivation of (19) employs the noncyclic application of Move (20b) (involving the elementary operations of both concatenation and replacement), whereas the cyclic derivation of (19) employs the cyclic application of Move (21a) (involving the elementary operation of concatenation only). Given this, the SDC ensures that the cyclic derivation of (19) with one elementary operation fewer wins over the noncyclic derivation of (19).

The same analysis holds for the relevant derivations of (25). Consider the deviant (25) and the relevant aspects of its noncyclic and cyclic derivations, given in (26) and (27), repeated here.

(25) ??Who$_2$ did you say that [pictures of t$_2$]$_1$ were stolen t$_1$?

(26) a. $[_{CP}$ who $[_{C'}$ C_{wh} $[_{IP}$ you said

       $[_{CP}$ that $[_{IP}$ were stolen $[_\alpha$ pictures of t(who)]]]]]]

    b. $[_{CP}$ who $[_{C'}$ C_{wh} $[_{IP}$ you said

       $[_{CP}$ that $[_{IP}[_\alpha$ pictures of t(who)] were stolen t(α)]]]]]

(27) a. $[_{IP}[_\alpha$ pictures of who] were stolen t(α)]

    b. $[_{CP}$ who $[_{C'}$ C_{wh} $[_{IP}$ you said

       $[_{CP}$ that $[_{IP}[_\alpha$ pictures of t(who)] were stolen t(α)]]]]]

The noncyclic derivation of (25) employs the noncyclic application of Move (26b) (involving the elementary operations of both concatenation and replacement), whereas the cyclic derivation of (25) employs the cyclic application of Move (27a) (involving the elementary operation of concatenation only). Given this, the SDC ensures that the cyclic derivation of (25) with one elementary operation fewer wins over the noncyclic derivation of (25).

Under the SDC analysis, therefore, the selected derivations—namely, the cyclic derivation of (19) and the cyclic derivation of (25)—violate the MLC and the Subject Condition, respectively.[14]

To summarize, the SDC determines the choice between cyclic and noncyclic overt applications of Move. The SDC analysis captures the "strict cyclicity" property of overt movement, thereby making tenable the simpler formulation of the SFC given in (35).[15]

2.3   Deriving Procrastinate

In the preceding sections, Merge and Move are understood in terms of
the elementary operations of concatenation and replacement. In this section, the only other operation of C_{HL}—namely, Erase—is examined with
particular attention to a relation between overt movement and covert
erasure. Given such a relation (to be made precise below), the central
cases motivating Procrastinate are shown to be deducible from the SDC.

2.3.1   Erasure = Replacement
In addition to the structure-building operations Merge and Move, C_{HL}
incorporates the third operation Erase, formulated as (37) (Chomsky
1995, 280).

(37)   *Erase*
       Applied to the category Σ with α containing F, Erase forms Σ' by
       replacing F in α by the empty element $\emptyset$.

Erase is an instance of the elementary operation of replacement, which is
defined so as to operate on a single phrase marker and to apply at the
nonroot (noncyclic application). Erase applies to the object Σ and forms
the new object Σ'. The output of this application is Σ' (i.e., Σ' is substituted
for Σ). The empty element $\emptyset$ is taken to be an actual symbol of mental
representation with no feature. The replacement of F by the empty element $\emptyset$ means that F is eliminated; hence, F is inaccessible to any further
operation (not just to interpretability at the interfaces). Suppose C_{HL} has
constructed the category Σ with a term α containing a feature F. Then,
Erase replaces F in α by the empty element $\emptyset$, forming Σ'.

(38)   Input: Σ (with α containing F)
       _____

       Replace F in α by the empty element $\emptyset$, forming Σ'
       _____

       Output: Σ'

This (noncyclic) application of Erase is illustrated in (39).

(39)   a. Σ b. Σ'

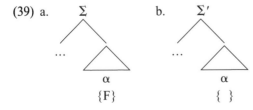

Given that Erase involves the elementary operation of replacement, the seemingly distinct operations Merge, Move, and Erase are now interpreted in terms of the elementary operations of concatenation and replacement (in the spirit of Lasnik and Saito's (1992) Affect α hypothesis). Consider (40).

(40) a. cyclic application of Merge ($=$ concatenation)
     b. cyclic application of Move ($=$ concatenation)
     c. noncyclic application of Merge ($=$ concatenation $+$ replacement)
     d. noncyclic application of Move ($=$ concatenation $+$ replacement)
     e. noncyclic application of Erase ($=$ replacement)

Under the SDC analysis, C_{HL} can perform any of (40a–e) but must minimize the number of elementary operations necessary for convergence. Given this, Erase applies to Σ only if some feature in Σ must be erased for convergence. Then, a question arises about what feature(s) must be erased for convergence.

First recall that a lexical item LI selected from a numeration N is a complex of (at most) three types of features: {PF[LI], SF[LI], FF[LI]}, where PF[LI] is the component of phonetic features of LI that serve only to yield π, SF[LI] is the component of semantic features of LI that serve only to yield λ, and FF[LI] is the component of formal features of LI that enter into a computation. Suppose Move raises LI in the overt syntax. Then, this application of Move leaves t(LI) ($=$ a complete copy of the moved LI) at the departure site, forming the chain CH (LI, t(LI)), more accurately represented as (41).

(41) CH ({PF[LI], SF[LI], FF[LI]}, t({PF[LI], SF[LI], FF[LI]}))

Under the theory of feature checking, the [−interpretable] features of FF[LI] (e.g., Case features) undergo checking and are erased immediately. The features of PF[LI] and SF[LI] (that are [+interpretable]) survive and are interpreted by the A-P system and the C-I system, respectively. Now suppose PF[LI] and SF[LI] are interpreted *only once*.[16] Then, the copying process (which resulted from the overt movement of LI = {PF[LI], SF[LI], FF[LI]}) induces erasure of PF[LI] and SF[LI] in either LI or t(LI) (to prevent PF[LI] and SF[LI] from being interpreted more than once). Given this natural relation between overt movement and covert erasure in the system, let us ask what role Erase plays to generate a legitimate pair (π, λ).

Suppose C_{HL} constructs the category Σ with the chain CH (α, t(α)), where α is an overt category with some semantic content. Then, Spell-Out applies to Σ and strips away from it those elements relevant only to π, leaving the residue Σ_L, which is mapped to λ. Σ is then mapped to π. In the LF component, Erase applies to Σ_L and replaces SF[α] in either α or t(α) by the empty element $\emptyset$, forming Σ'_L. In the PF component, on the other hand, all the features of α, except for PF[α] in the head of CH, are erased.[17] Pointing out that such massive erasure eliminates features in ways not permitted in the mapping of N to λ, Chomsky (1995) suggests that the mapping of Σ to π should be regarded as quite distinct from a computation from N to λ. Following his suggestion, I assume that Erase performs erasure in the mapping of N to λ, but it does not perform massive erasure in the mapping of Σ to π. Given this assumption, the SDC (minimizing the number of elementary operations necessary for convergence) constrains the number of applications of Erase in the mapping of N to λ, but whether or not derivational economy constrains massive erasure in the mapping of Σ to π is an open issue.[18]

Given these assumptions, let us examine how Erase functions to generate a legitimate LF object, say, an argument *John* in examples such as (42).

(42) The police arrested John.

Under the theory of feature movement, in the overt syntax, Move raises LI along with all the features of LI, whereas in the LF component, Move raises just FF[LI]. Given this, for the checking of the Case feature of *John* in the LF component, Move raises just FF[John] to the verb, leaving SF[John] behind. In the LF representation of (42), therefore, SF[John] is interpreted where *John* is θ-marked. Now compare (42) with (43), in which *John* undergoes overt movement.

(43) John was arrested by the police.

In the overt syntax, Move raises *John* along with all the features of *John*, forming the chain CH (John, t(John)). Assuming that SF[John] is interpreted only once at LF, SF[John] must be erased from either the head of CH or the tail of CH. Chomsky (1995, 359) proposes that "the forms that reach the LF level must be as similar as typological variation permits— unique, if that is possible," a proposal that he calls the *minimalist principle of poverty of interpretation at the interface*. Given this principle, in the LF representation of (43), SF[John] is interpreted where *John* is θ-marked (just like SF[John] in the LF representation of (42)). That is, in the LF component, Erase replaces SF[John] in the head of CH by the empty element $\emptyset$.

As shown above, the LF erasure of SF[LI] is necessary only when LI undergoes overt movement. The system proposed here incorporates this natural relation between the overt movement of LI with some semantic content and the covert erasure of SF[LI] given in (44).[19]

(44) Suppose LI is a category with some semantic content. Then, an overt application of Move forming CH (LI, t(LI)) induces an additional application of Erase eliminating SF[LI] from the head of CH.

In the following subsections, I argue that under the SDC analysis developed here, the empirical motivation for Procrastinate, an axiom governing the timing of verb movement, object shift, and expletive insertion, can be explained without any stipulation regarding pre- versus post-Spell-Out cost distinctions: Procrastinate can be eliminated from the Minimalist Program.

2.3.2 Deriving the Timing of Verb Movement

Within the theory of feature checking, a finite verb must invariably move to enter into a checking relation with T, but the timing of such verb movement may vary across languages. For example, the following contrasts suggest that French employs overt verb movement (see (45)), whereas English employs covert verb movement (see (46)):[20]

(45) a.   Jean embrasse souvent Marie.
     b. *Jean souvent embrasse Marie.

(46) a. *John kisses often Mary.
     b.   John often kisses Mary.

Suppose that adverbs such as *souvent* in (45) and *often* in (46) are generated within the v^{max}. Then, (45) shows that the raising of *embrasse* to T must be overt, whereas (46) shows that the raising of *kisses* to T must be postponed until the LF component. Suppose that overt verb movement to T is forced by the checking of the strong V-feature of T. Then, this crosslinguistic variation comes down to the strength of the V-feature of T: the V-feature of T is strong in French, but not in English. Given this, the timing of verb movement is (in part) determined by the Strong Feature Condition (SFC), repeated in (47).

(47) *Strong Feature Condition*
     Spell-Out applies to Σ only if Σ contains no category with a strong feature.

Given that the V-feature of T is strong in French, the SFC forces the application of Move raising V to T to take place before Spell-Out. Now notice that the derivation of (45a) satisfies the SFC, but the derivation of (45b) does not. Consider the following structures of (45a–b) to which Spell-Out applies:[21,22]

(48) a. [$_{CP}$[$_{TP}$ Jean [embrasse + v] + T [$_{vP}$ souvent t(v)
           [$_{VP}$ t(embrasse) Marie]]]]

      b. [$_{CP}$[$_{TP}$ Jean T [$_{vP}$ souvent embrasse+v
           [$_{VP}$ t(embrasse) Marie]]]]

Spell-Out applying to (48a) satisfies the SFC because T bears no strong feature: subject raising and verb movement have checked all the strong features of T. By contrast, Spell-Out applying to (48b) violates the SFC because T still bears the strong V-feature: verb movement has not yet occurred. As shown above, the SFC determines the choice between overt and covert verb movement in French: the SFC permits the derivation of (45a) (employing overt verb movement), and it excludes the derivation of (45b) (employing covert verb movement).

In English, on the other hand, T bears no strong V-feature attracting V; hence, Spell-Out can apply to the following structures of (46a–b) without violating the SFC:

(49) a. [$_{CP}$[$_{TP}$ John [kisses + v] + T [$_{vP}$ often t(v) [$_{VP}$ t(kisses) Mary]]]]

      b. [$_{CP}$[$_{TP}$ John T [$_{vP}$ often kisses + v [$_{VP}$ t(kisses) Mary]]]]

Spell-Out applying to (49a–b) satisfies the SFC because T bears no strong feature: T bears no strong V-feature, and subject raising has checked the strong D-feature of T. That is, the SFC forces overt verb movement in French, but not in English. A question arises about why verb movement (not forced by the SFC) must be postponed until LF.

To postpone verb movement (not forced by the SFC) until the LF component, Chomsky (1993, 30) appeals to the principle Procrastinate, repeated in (50).

(50) *Procrastinate*
      Minimize the number of overt operations necessary for convergence.

In English, overt verb movement is not forced by the SFC (i.e., its covert counterpart would allow convergence). Given this, Procrastinate ensures that the derivation of (46a) with overt verb movement is blocked by the derivation of (46b) with covert verb movement because the former employs one overt operation more. Procrastinate (stipulating the preference for a covert operation over an overt one) is thus empirically motivated.

I argue, however, within the analysis incorporating the Shortest Derivation Condition (SDC), that the selection of the derivation of (46b) over the derivation of (46a) can be deduced without any reference to the pre- versus post-Spell-Out cost distinctions stipulated in Procrastinate. The SDC is repeated in (51).

(51) *Shortest Derivation Condition*
Minimize the number of elementary operations necessary for convergence.

Recall that under the theory of feature movement, overt verb movement raises not just FF[V] but also the other two components of interface features, PF[V] and SF[V], whereas covert verb movement raises only FF[V]. Under the copy theory of movement, overt verb movement leaves a copy of all three components of V, whereas covert verb movement leaves a copy of FF[V] only.

Suppose Move overtly raises V, forming the chain CH (V, t(V)), Spell-Out strips PF[V] from both V and t(V), and SF[V] is interpreted only once where V assigns a θ-role to its argument(s). Then, this overt application of Move, unlike its covert counterpart, induces at least one additional application of Erase that eliminates SF[V] from the head of CH in the LF component. Now notice that both the overt application of Move raising V and its covert counterpart involve the elementary operations of concatenation and replacement, but the former (not the latter) induces an additional application of Erase that involves the elementary operation of replacement. Under the SDC analysis, therefore, the derivation of (46a) with overt verb movement is blocked by the derivation of (46b) with covert verb movement because the former employs one elementary operation more. The SDC determines the choice between overt and covert verb movement in English, and it does so without any reference to Procrastinate.

As shown above, in French, the SFC forces overt verb movement for checking of the strong V-feature of T. In English, the SDC determines the timing of verb movement: overt verb movement that raises all three feature components of V (which induces an additional application of Erase) is blocked by its covert counterpart that raises only FF[V]. The preference for covert operations over overt ones (stipulated in Procrastinate) thus follows naturally from the SDC.

2.3.3 Deriving the Timing of Object Shift

In this subsection, I show that the timing of object shift is captured by the SDC analysis. First consider the following contrast:

(52) a.   John kisses Mary.
     b.   *John Mary kisses.

(52) shows that object shift must be postponed until the LF component in English, which suggests that the English light verb v bears no strong feature attracting Obj. Now consider the following structures of (52a–b) to which Spell-Out applies:

(53) a. $[_{CP}[_{TP}$ John $[_{vP}$ kisses $+ v$ $[_{VP}$ t(kisses) Mary]]]]
     b. $[_{CP}[_{TP}$ John $[_{vP}$ Mary kisses $+ v$ $[_{VP}$ t(kisses) t(Mary)]]]]

Given that (53a–b) contain no category with a strong feature, Spell-Out can apply to them without violating the SFC: the SFC does not determine the timing of object shift in English. To ensure the postponement of object shift (not forced by the SFC) until the LF component, we appeal to two independently motivated principles: the MLC and the SDC.

Recall first that overt object shift (cyclic application of Move) employs the elementary operation of concatenation, whereas covert object shift (noncyclic application of Move) employs the elementary operations of concatenation and replacement. Second, overt object shift raises not just FF[Obj] but also the other two components of the interface features of Obj, namely, PF[Obj] and SF[Obj]; hence, a complete copy of these three components of Obj is left behind. By contrast, covert object shift raises just FF[Obj]; hence, a copy of only FF[Obj] is left behind. Now suppose Move overtly raises Obj, forming the chain CH (Obj, t(Obj)), Spell-Out strips PF[Obj] from both Obj and t(Obj), and SF[Obj] is interpreted only once where CH is assigned a θ-role. Then, this overt application of Move, unlike its covert counterpart, induces an application of Erase that employs the elementary operation of replacement.

Given the discussion above, the SDC seemingly permits overt object shift as well as covert object shift in English, contrary to fact: the derivations of (52a–b) are equally economical since these two derivations employ the same "minimal" number of elementary operations to converge. However, although the derivation of (52b) may not induce an extra step, overt object shift without overt verb movement yields a structure in which the MLC prohibits T from attracting Subj in the overt syntax (see, among others, Holmberg 1986; Jonas 1995, 1996, Jonas and Bobaljik

1993; Thráinsson 1993).[23] Let us examine the relevant aspects of the derivation of (52b).

At some point in the derivation, C_{HL} constructs (54).

(54)

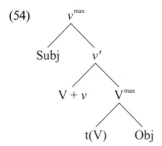

As the next step, Move raises Obj to the outer specifier of v (to which V is already adjoined), forming (55).

(55)

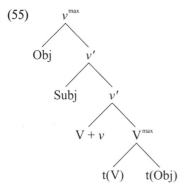

Then, Merge concatenates T and v^{max}, forming (56).

(56)

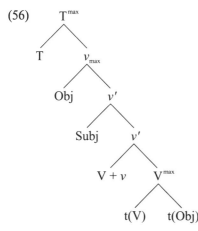

Finally, Move raises Subj to the specifier of T (to which the complex head
$V + v$ has not yet been adjoined), forming (57).

(57)

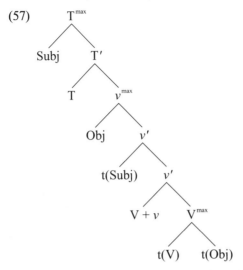

This application of Move violates the Minimal Link Condition (MLC),
repeated in (58).

(58) *Minimal Link Condition*
    H(K) attracts α only if there is no β, β closer to H(K) than α, such
    that H(K) attracts β.

Recall the notion "closer," repeated in (59).

(59) β is closer to H(K) than α iff β c-commands α, and β is not in the
    minimal domain of CH, where CH is the chain headed by γ, and γ
    is adjoined to H(K).

In (56), Obj is not in the minimal domain of CH the head of which is
adjoined to T, and Obj c-commands Subj; hence, Obj is closer to T
than Subj. Given this, the MLC prohibits T from attracting Subj in
mapping (56) to (57): the MLC excludes the derivation of (52b), as
desired.

    Suppose C_{HL} raises the complex head $V + v$ to T, forming (60) (in-
stead of (56)) and raises Subj to the specifier of T, forming (61) (instead
of (57)).

(60)
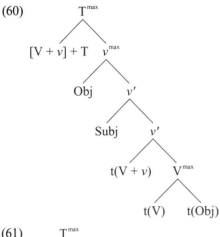

(61)
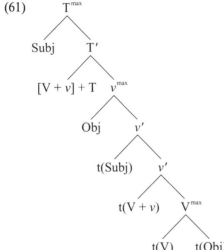

In (60), Obj is in the minimal domain of CH (V + v, t(V + v)) the head of which is adjoined to T; hence, Obj does not prevent T from attracting Subj in mapping (60) to (61). Thus, Move raises Subj to the specifier of T without violating the MLC. This is the MLC analysis of Holmberg's (1986) generalization: a derivation D involving overt object shift induces a violation of the MLC unless D involves overt verb movement prior to subject raising.

As we saw in subsection 2.3.2, overt verb movement necessarily yields a less economical derivation in English. Given this, the SDC excludes this alternative derivation involving overt verb movement and overt object shift. Thus, given the MLC and the SDC, C_{HL} selects the derivation of (52a) involving covert verb movement and covert object shift as the optimal convergent derivation.

We have thus reached the conclusions that (a) unless the verb overtly moves to T, overt object shift yields a structure in which the MLC prohibits T from attracting Subj, and (b) the SDC ensures the postponement of verb movement (unforced by the SFC) until the LF component: the SDC excludes any derivation involving (unforced) overt verb movement in English. That is, the SDC selects the derivation of (52a) involving covert object shift and covert verb movement as the shortest derivation, and the MLC excludes the derivation of (52b) involving overt object shift and covert verb movement. Therefore, the timing of object shift in English follows without any reference to the pre- versus post-Spell-Out cost distinctions stipulated in Procrastinate.

Under the SDC analysis, therefore, the postponement of verb movement until the LF component entails the postponement of object shift until the LF component. If this is the case, we expect that languages with overt verb movement may exhibit "optional" overt object shift. Icelandic appears to be one such language (see, among others, Holmberg 1986; Jonas and Bobaljik 1993; Thráinsson 1993). Consider the following Icelandic pair, which shows that overt verb movement is obligatory, whereas overt object shift is optional:[24,25]

(62) a. Risarnir átu [$_{vP}$ ekki t(átu) ríkisstjórnia].
       the-giants ate   not   the-government
       'The giants did not eat the government.'

   b. Risarnir átu ríkisstjórnia   [$_{vP}$ ekki t(átu) t(ríkisstjórnia)].
      the-giants ate the-government   not

Given that the adverb *ekki* is generated inside the v^{max} (Jonas 1992, 1995, 1996), the Icelandic finite verb (unlike the English finite verb) invariably undergoes overt movement to T. Under the SFC analysis, the Icelandic finite verb moves to check the strong V-feature of T in the overt syntax.

As for optional overt object shift, Chomsky (1995, 352) assumes that the Icelandic light verb v is optionally assigned the strong D-feature. But this assumption (incorporated into the system to account for (62b)) is simply a restatement of the optionality problem. This is an undesirable consequence of the Procrastinate analysis, under which unforced overt operations are (uniformly) excluded. Thus, this type of optionality is not permitted unless "optional" movement is restated as "optional" feature strength triggering such (obligatory) movement.

Under the SDC analysis, however, a principled account of optionality is possible, which requires neither Procrastinate nor optional feature strength. Let us examine the structures of (62a–b), schematically represented as (63a–b), respectively.

(63) a. $[_{CP}[_{TP}$ Subj $[V + v] + T$ $[_{vP}$ adv t(Subj) t(v)
$[_{VP}$ t(V) Obj]]]]

    b. $[_{CP}[_{TP}$ Subj $[V + v] + T$ $[_{vP}$ Obj adv t(Subj) t(v)
$[_{VP}$ t(V) t(Obj)]]]]

In the derivation of (62a), Obj stays in situ in the overt syntax, yielding (63a). Later, in the LF component, Move raises FF[Obj]. This covert noncyclic application of Move, involving the elementary operations of concatenation and replacement, induces no additional application of Erase. In the derivation of (62b), Move raises Obj to the outer specifier of v in the overt syntax, yielding (63b). This overt cyclic application of Move, involving the elementary operation of concatenation, induces the covert application of Erase, involving the elementary operation of replacement (which eliminates SF[Obj] from the head of CH). The Icelandic finite verb invariably moves to T; hence, T can attract Subj whether or not Obj is shifted to the specifier of v (see the mapping from (60) to (61)). Therefore, these two derivations employ the same "minimal" number of elementary operations to converge: they are equally economical derivations. Under the SDC analysis, therefore, the choice between overt and covert object shift in Icelandic has no consequence in the eyes of derivational economy: object shift can be optionally overt, as exhibited by (62a–b).

The proposed analysis of optional object shift is further supported by the following contrast (cited from Thráinsson 1993):

(64) a. Risarnir hafa $[_{vP}$ ekki étið ríkisstjórnia].
      the-giants have   not eaten the-government.
      'The giants have not eaten the government.'

    b. *Risarnir hafa ríkisstjórnia $[_{vP}$ ekki étið t(ríkisstjórnia)].
      the-giants have the-government   not eaten

The Icelandic nonfinite verb does not undergo overt movement. In (64a–b), the strong V-feature of T is arguably checked by the auxiliary *hafa*; consequently, the nonfinite verb remains inside the v^{max} in the overt syntax. Recall again that unless the verb overtly moves to T, overt object shift yields a structure in which the MLC prohibits T from attracting Subj in the overt syntax. Given this analysis, let us consider the structures of (64a–b), schematically represented as (65a–b).

(65) a. $[_{CP}[_{TP}$ Subj Aux + T $[_{vP}$ adv t(Subj) V + v $[_{VP}$ t(V) Obj]]]]]
    b. $[_{CP}[_{TP}$ Subj Aux + T $[_{vP}$ Obj adv t(Subj) V + v $[_{VP}$ t(V) t(Obj)]]]]]

Unlike the derivation of (64a) (yielding (65a)), the derivation of (64b) (yielding (65b)) employs overt object shift and yields a structure in which overt subject raising violates the MLC. Obj is not in the minimal domain of CH the head of which is adjoined to T, and Obj c-commands Subj; hence, Obj is closer to T than Subj. Given this, the MLC prohibits T from attracting Subj, thereby excluding the derivation of (64b), as desired.

We have seen so far that the timing of verb movement and object shift is deducible from the morphological properties of T: (a) overt verb movement is forced by the SFC if T bears the strong V-feature and attracts V (see French (45a–b)), (b) covert verb movement is forced by the SDC if T bears no strong V-feature (see English (46a–b)), (c) overt object shift (preceding overt subject raising) is in effect prohibited by the MLC if T bears no strong V-feature (see English (52a–b)), or T bears the strong V-feature but attracts Aux (rather than V) (see Icelandic (64a–b)), and (d) optional overt object shift is permitted by the SDC if T bears the strong V-feature and attracts V (see Icelandic (62a–b)).[26]

2.3.4 Deriving the Timing of Expletive Insertion

In this subsection, I show that the timing of expletive insertion can be deduced from the SDC. Consider the following contrast in English (cited from Chomsky 1994, 1995):

(66) a. There$_1$ seems $[_{TP}$ t$_1$ to be someone in the room].
    b. *There seems $[_{TP}$ someone$_1$ to be t$_1$ in the room].

In the derivation of (66a), the expletive *there* is inserted in the specifier of the embedded T to check the strong D-feature of the embedded T; and later in the derivation, *there* is raised to the specifier of the matrix T to check the strong D-feature of the matrix T. In the derivation of (66b), *someone* is raised to the specifier of the embedded T to check the strong D-feature of the embedded T; and later in the derivation, *there* is inserted in the specifier of the matrix T to check the strong D-feature of the matrix

T. Given that these derivations (associated with the same initial numeration) satisfy all the morphological properties, they compete in the eyes of derivational economy.

Chomsky (1994; 1995, 346) argues that Procrastinate forces C_{HL} to select the derivation of (66a) over the derivation of (66b). Let us first examine his proposal. Consider the following structure that is common to the two derivations:

(67) [$_{TP}$ to be someone in the room]

The next step must fill the specifier of T to check the strong D-feature of T. Given the initial numeration, there are two possibilities: C_{HL} can insert *there* in the specifier of T or raise *someone* to this position. Chomsky interprets Procrastinate to mean that overt movement must be postponed as late as possible even in the overt syntax, and he argues that Procrastinate applies to this stage of the derivation, forcing C_{HL} to select the first option over the second one (which involves overt movement unforced by the SFC). The first option yields (68).

(68) [$_{TP}$ there [$_{T'}$ to be someone in the room]]

At a later stage in the derivation, C_{HL} reaches the following structure:

(69) [$_{TP}$ seems [$_{TP}$ there [$_{T'}$ to be someone in the room]]]

The next step must fill the specifier of the matrix T to check the strong D-feature of the matrix T. The MLC forces C_{HL} to raise *there*, given that *there* is closer to the matrix T than *someone*. C_{HL} raises *there* to the specifier of the matrix T, forming (70).

(70) [$_{TP}$ there [$_{T'}$ seems [$_{TP}$ t(there) [$_{T'}$ to be someone in the room]]]]

Under Chomsky's (1994, 1995) framework, therefore, Procrastinate (with his interpretation) selects the derivation that involves the insertion of *there* in the specifier of the embedded T: the derivation of (66a) blocks the derivation of (66b).[27]

The timing of expletive insertion, exhibited here, also follows from the SDC analysis, without invoking any particular interpretation of Procrastinate. First consider the lexical property of a (pure) expletive Exp such as *there*, given in (71) (Chomsky 1995, 364).

(71) Exp is a phonetically overt but semantically vacuous category, which contains the categorial feature [D] that checks the strong D-feature of T.

Assuming (71), we take Exp to be a complex of two types of features: {PF[Exp], FF[Exp]}, where FF[Exp] contains just the categorial feature [D].[28,29] Suppose Move raises Exp in the overt syntax. Then, the chain CH (Exp, t(Exp)) is formed. Later, Spell-Out strips away the phonological properties of CH, forming (72).

(72) CH (FF[Exp], t(FF[Exp]))

(72) shows that the overt movement of a semantically vacuous category (e.g., *there*) induces no additional application of Erase (which would eliminate SF[there] from the head of CH). But recall that the overt movement of a category with some semantic content (e.g., *someone*) induces (at least) one additional application of Erase (which eliminates SF[someone] from the head of CH). Keeping in mind this natural consequence of the irreducible lexical difference, let us once again examine the relevant aspects of the derivations of (66a–b), repeated here.

(66) a. There$_1$ seems [$_{TP}$ t$_1$ to be someone in the room].
      b. *There seems [$_{TP}$ someone$_1$ to be t$_1$ in the room].

The crucial difference between the derivation of (66a) and the derivation of (66b) is that the former involves the overt movement of *there* to the specifier of the matrix T, whereas the latter involves the overt movement of *someone* to the specifier of the embedded T. Given the irreducible lexical difference between the semantically vacuous category *there* and the category with some semantic content *someone*, the overt movement of *someone* (in the derivation of (66b)), unlike the overt movement of *there* (in the derivation of (66a)), induces at least one additional application of Erase (which eliminates SF[someone] from the head of CH). Under the SDC analysis, therefore, the derivation of (66a) with one elementary operation fewer blocks the derivation of (66b): the SDC captures the timing of expletive insertion in English.

To summarize, the SDC analysis, dispensing with Procrastinate, ensures that a derivation D selects the overt movement of a semantically vacuous category (e.g., *there*) over the overt movement of a category with some semantic content (e.g., *someone*) if such selection allows D to converge.

2.3.5 On the Intuitive Idea behind Procrastinate
The central cases motivating Procrastinate have been shown to be explicable without any reference to pre- versus post-Spell-Out cost distinctions.

In this subsection, I will discuss the intuitive idea behind Procrastinate in light of the SDC analysis.

Chomsky (1993, 30) states the intuitive idea behind Procrastinate as follows.

(73) The intuitive idea is that LF operations are a kind of "wired-in" reflex, operating mechanically beyond any directly observable effects. They are less costly than overt operations.

This intuitive idea raises the following two intimately related questions:

(74) a. What does it mean that LF operations are a kind of "wired-in" reflex?

    b. Why is it the case that LF operations are less costly than overt ones?

Under the Minimalist Program explored here, these questions are answered on principled grounds. Let us consider them in turn.

(74a) is answered by the theory of feature movement. Under this theory, the "wired-in" operation is Move F, which raises FF[F]. In the overt syntax, however, Move F does not raise just FF[F]. Chomsky (1995) suggests that isolated features and other scattered parts of words induce a violation of the interface conditions imposed by the A-P system: they are simply unpronounceable. Thus, in the overt syntax, C_{HL} raises the minimal category containing FF[F] that allows convergence. In the LF component, however, being free from the A-P interface conditions, C_{HL} raises just FF[F]. In this sense, LF operations, unlike overt ones, are a kind of "wired-in" reflex.

(74b) is answered by the copy theory of movement and the SDC. Suppose α is a category with some semantic content and C_{HL} raises α in the overt syntax. Then, under the copy theory of movement, this overt application of Move raising α forms the chain CH (α, t(α)) (where t(α) is a complete copy of α), thereby inducing (at least) one additional covert application of Erase (which eliminates the component of SF[α] from the head of CH). If the raising of α is postponed until the LF component, then C_{HL} raises just FF[α]. This covert application of Move raising just FF[α] induces no additional application of Erase. In this sense, LF operations are less costly than overt ones. Given this natural relation between overt movement and covert erasure, we can eliminate Procrastinate (requiring the number of overt operations necessary for convergence to be minimized): the SDC (requiring the number of elementary operations necessary for convergence to be minimized) postpones overt movement until the LF component if such postponement allows convergence.[30]

2.4 Summary

In this chapter, I unified the seemingly discrete operations Merge, Move, and Erase as instances of the elementary operations of concatenation and replacement. Given this unification, I proposed that a derivation D employs the fewest number of the elementary operations to converge, and that such minimization of the length of D is ensured by the Shortest Derivation Condition (SDC), repeated in (75).

(75) *Shortest Derivation Condition*
Minimize the number of elementary operations necessary for convergence.

As an immediate consequence of this proposal, I showed that the SDC captures the "strict cyclicity" properties of merger and overt movement. Furthermore, I demonstrated that Procrastinate can be eliminated from the Minimalist Program: the SDC determines the timing of verb movement, object shift, and expletive insertion without any reference to pre-versus post-Spell-Out cost distinctions (stipulated in Procrastinate).

2.5 Appendix: Expletives and Multiple-Subject Constructions

Chomsky (1995) examines the timing of expletive insertion in other constructions. Consider the following Icelandic examples (cited from Jonas 1995, 1996):

(76) a. það   hafa margir jólasveinar   borðað búðinginn.
        there have many Christmas-trolls eaten   the-pudding
        'Many Christmas trolls have eaten the pudding.'
     b. það   hafa nokkrar kökur verið bakaðar fyrir veisluna.
        there have some   cakes been baked   for   the-party
        'Some cakes have been baked for the party.'

Chomsky refers to constructions such as (76a–b) as *multiple-subject constructions* (MSCs). In such constructions, the head T is taken to be a category projecting two specifiers: one is for Exp; the other is for Subj. The property of T projecting ≥ 2 specifiers is characterized as follows (adapted from Chomsky 1995, 354):

(77) In languages such as Icelandic (unlike other languages such as English), T is assigned the strong D-feature with an option to escape erasure when checked.

An MSC results if this option is exercised. Icelandic can exercise this option (at most) once. When this option is exercised, C_{HL} must check the strong D-feature of T twice; hence, T must project two specifiers.[31] Under this proposal, (76a–b) are assigned the following structures (with English words):[32]

(78) a. $[_{CP}[_{TP}$ there have + T $[_{T'}$ many Christmas trolls
       $[_{vP}$ eaten the pudding]]]]]
   b. $[_{CP}[_{TP}$ there have + T $[_{T'}$ some cakes
       $[_{vP}$ been baked for the party]]]]]

In (78a–b), Exp occupies the outer specifier of T, whereas Subj occupies the inner specifier of T. As Chomsky (1995, 368) notes, this multiple-specifier analysis predicts the wrong order of elements. The observed order is (79a), whereas the predicted one is (79b).

(79) a. Exp–T–Subj–vP
   b. Exp–Subj–T–vP

Chomsky suggests that the real order (in the $N \rightarrow \lambda$ computation) is (79b), assuming that the observed order (79a) is formed by PF operations (which are extraneous to the $N \rightarrow \lambda$ computation). Following his suggestion, I assume that the order is really (79b), irrespective of what is observed at the PF output.

   Chomsky (1995, sec. 4.10) extends his multiple-specifier analysis to the following Icelandic example (cited from Jonas 1995, 1996).

(80) það   virðist einhver vera   í herberginu.
    there seems someone be.INF in the-room
    'There seems to be someone in the room.'

The multiple-specifier analysis assigns to (80) the following two distinct structures (with English words):

(81) a. $[_{CP}[_{TP}$ there seems $[_{T'}$ someone ... $[_{TP}$ t' (someone) to be
       t(someone) in the room]]]]]

b. [$_{CP}$[$_{TP}$ there seems . . . [$_{TP}$ t(there) [$_{T'}$ someone to be
t(someone) in the room]]]]

In (81a), the matrix clause is an MSC: *there* occupies the outer specifier of
the matrix T, whereas the raised *someone* occupies the inner specifier of
the matrix T. The embedded TP is the complement of the matrix verb
seems (and the displacement of *seems* occurs in the PF component).
The intermediate trace of *someone*—namely, *t'(someone)*—occupies the
specifier of the embedded T. The structure of (81a) (to which Spell-Out
applies) is illustrated in (82).

(82)

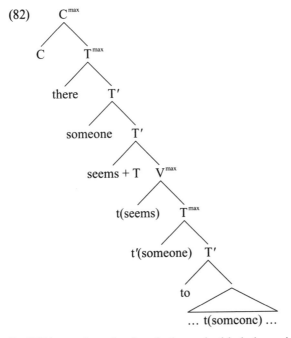

In (81b), on the other hand, the embedded clause is an MSC: the trace of
there—namely, *t(there)*—occupies the outer specifier of the embedded T,
whereas the raised *someone* occupies the inner specifier of the embedded
T. The raised *there* occupies the specifier of the matrix T. The structure of
(81b) (to which Spell-Out applies) is illustrated in (83).

(83)

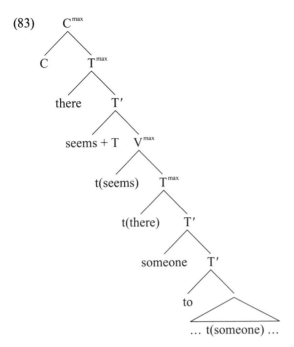

The structures of (81a–b) given in (82) and (83) appear to be legitimate (Chomsky 1995; Jonas 1995, 1996).

Now compare Icelandic (81a–b) with English (66a–b), repeated in (84a–b).

(84) a. There$_1$ seems [$_{TP}$ t$_1$ to be someone in the room].
  b. *There seems [$_{TP}$ someone$_1$ to be t$_1$ in the room].

The English T cannot escape erasure when checked. Given this assumption, the SDC analysis forces C$_{HL}$ to introduce *there* into a derivation as early as possible, ensuring the insertion of *there* in the specifier of the embedded T: the derivation of (84a) blocks the derivation of (84b). The Icelandic T, however, has an option to escape erasure when checked. The matrix T of (81a) and the embedded T of (81b) each exercise this option once and project two specifiers. Given this, the derivations of (81a–b) each exhibit the insertion of *there* in the outer specifier of T projecting two specifiers.

In this appendix, I argue that the insertion of *there* in the outer specifier of T projecting two specifiers (in such languages as Icelandic) is ensured by convergence considerations. That is, given the initial numeration N of

(81a–b), all their competitors (associated with N) that insert *there* in some position other than the outer specifier of T projecting two specifiers are shown to be excluded as nonconvergent derivations (irrelevant to the SDC).

First consider the relevant aspects of the derivation of (81a). At some point in the derivation, C_{HL} constructs the following structure, whose head T requires a single specifier:

(85) [$_{TP}$ to be someone in the room]

The next step fills the specifier of T to check the strong D-feature of T. Given the initial numeration, there are two possibilities: C_{HL} can insert *there* in the specifier of T or raise *someone* to this position. Suppose the first option is selected. Then, C_{HL} inserts *there* in the specifier of T, forming (86).

(86) [$_{TP}$ there [$_{T'}$ to be someone in the room]]

At a later stage in the derivation, C_{HL} reaches the following structure, whose head T requires two specifiers:

(87) [$_{TP}$ seems + T [$_{VP}$ t(seems) [$_{TP}$ there [$_{T'}$ to be someone in the room]]]]

Recall that the matrix T of (81a), assigned the strong D-feature with an option to escape erasure when checked, exercises this option once: the matrix T must undergo the checking of its strong D-feature twice, thereby requiring two specifiers. Given this, the next step fills the (inner) specifier of the matrix T. The matrix T attracts a category in the way permitted by the computational principles. Recall the MLC and the definition of closeness, repeated in (88) and (89).

(88) *Minimal Link Condition*
   H(K) attracts α only if there is no β, β closer to H(K) than α, such that H(K) attracts β.

(89) β is closer to H(K) than α iff β c-commands α, and β is not in the minimal domain of CH, where CH is the chain headed by γ, and γ is adjoined to H(K).

In (87), *there* is not in the minimal domain of CH the head of which is adjoined to the matrix T, and *there* c-commands *someone*; hence, *there* is closer to the matrix T than *someone*. Given this, the MLC prohibits the matrix T from attracting *someone*; consequently, C_{HL} raises *there* to the (inner) specifier of the matrix T, forming (90).

(90) [$_{TP}$ there [$_{T'}$ seems + T [$_{VP}$ t(seems) [$_{TP}$ t(there) [$_{T'}$ to be someone in the room]]]]]]

The next step fills the outer specifier of the matrix T to complete the checking of the strong D-feature of the matrix T. C_{HL} performs a procedure in accordance with the C-Command Condition, repeated in (91).

(91) *C-Command Condition*
     H(K) attracts α only if H(K) c-commands α.

Given that the matrix T does not c-command *there*, the C-Command Condition prohibits it from attracting *there*; consequently, C_{HL} raises *someone* to the outer specifier of the matrix T, forming (92).[33]

(92) [$_{TP}$ someone [$_{T'}$ there [$_{T'}$ seems + T [$_{VP}$ t(seems) [$_{TP}$ t(there) [$_{T'}$ to be t(someone) in the room]]]]]]]

This derivation later yields an LF structure in which *there* in the inner specifier of the matrix T fails to c-command its associate *someone* in the outer specifier of the matrix T. Chomsky (1995, 373) excludes such an LF structure. He argues that the categorial feature [D] of the expletive undergoes erasure when the N-feature of its associate adjoins to it (Longobardi 1994), and such erasure is necessary for convergence. Given this convergence condition, the derivation yielding (92) fails to converge: the C-Command Condition prohibits the expletive *there* from attracting its associate *someone*; consequently, the D-feature of *there* survives intact to LF.[34,35]

The fatal step was made in mapping (85) to (86). Suppose the second option is selected. Then, C_{HL} raises *someone* to the specifier of T, forming (93) (instead of (86)).

(93) [$_{TP}$ someone [$_{T'}$ to be t(someone) in the room]]

At a later stage in the derivation, C_{HL} reaches the following structure, whose head T requires two specifiers:

(94) [$_{TP}$ seems + T [$_{VP}$ t(seems) [$_{TP}$ someone [$_{T'}$ to be t(someone) in the room]]]]

The next step fills the (inner) specifier of the matrix T. Given the initial numeration, there are two possibilities: C_{HL} can insert *there* in the (inner) specifier of the matrix T or raise *someone* to this position. Suppose the first option is selected. Then, C_{HL} inserts *there* in the (inner) specifier of T, forming (95).

(95) [$_{TP}$ there [$_{T'}$ seems + T [$_{VP}$ t(seems) [$_{TP}$ someone [$_{T'}$ to be t(someone) in the room]]]]]

The next step fills the outer specifier of the matrix T to complete the checking of the strong D-feature of the matrix T. The C-Command Condition prohibits the matrix T from attracting *there*; consequently, C_{HL} raises *someone* to the outer specifier of the matrix T, forming (96).

(96) [$_{TP}$ someone [$_{T'}$ there [$_{T'}$ seems + T [$_{VP}$ t(seems) [$_{TP}$ t′(someone) [$_{T'}$ to be t(someone) in the room]]]]]]

This derivation later yields an LF structure in which *there* in the inner specifier of the matrix T fails to c-command its associate *someone* in the outer specifier of the matrix T. The C-Command Condition prohibits *there* from attracting *someone*, and consequently, the D-feature of *there* survives intact to LF. The derivation yielding (96), just like the derivation yielding (92), fails to converge.

The fatal step was made in mapping (94) to (95). Suppose the second option is selected. Then, C_{HL} raises *someone* to the (inner) specifier of the matrix T, forming (97) (instead of (95)).

(97) [$_{TP}$ someone [$_{T'}$ seems + T [$_{VP}$ t(seems) [$_{TP}$ t′(someone) [$_{T'}$ to be t(someone) in the room]]]]]

The next step fills the outer specifier of the matrix T to complete the checking of the strong D-feature of the matrix T. Given that the matrix T cannot attract *someone*, C_{HL} inserts the remaining expletive *there* in the outer specifier of the matrix T, forming (98).

(98) [$_{TP}$ there [$_{T'}$ someone [$_{T'}$ seems + T [$_{VP}$ t(seems) [$_{TP}$ t′(someone) [$_{T'}$ to be t(someone) in the room]]]]]]

In (98), *there* in the outer specifier of the matrix T c-commands its associate *someone* in the inner specifier of the matrix T; hence, *there* can attract *someone*. In the LF component, C_{HL} adjoins the N-feature of *someone* to *there*; consequently, the D-feature of *there* undergoes erasure. The resulting LF structure satisfies all the morphological properties: the derivation yielding (98), unlike other derivations, converges. We have thus reached the following conclusion: for any derivation D associated with the initial numeration of (81a), D fails to converge if D inserts *there* in some position other than the outer specifier of T projecting two specifiers. That is, the insertion of *there* in the outer specifier of the matrix T of (81a) is required for convergence.

The same analysis holds for the derivation of (81b). Consider the relevant aspects of the derivation of (81b). At some point in the derivation, C_{HL} constructs the following structure, whose head T requires two specifiers:

(99) [$_{TP}$ to be someone in the room]

Recall that the embedded T of (81b), assigned the strong D-feature with an option to escape erasure when checked, exercises this option once: the embedded T must undergo the checking of its strong D-feature twice, thereby requiring two specifiers. Given this, the next step fills the (inner) specifier of T. Given the initial numeration, there are two possibilities: C_{HL} can insert *there* in the (inner) specifier of T or raise *someone* to this position. Suppose the first option is selected. Then, C_{HL} inserts *there* in the (inner) specifier of T, forming (100).

(100) [$_{TP}$ there [$_{T'}$ to be someone in the room]]

The next step fills the outer specifier of T to complete the checking of the strong D-feature of T. The C-Command Condition prohibits T from attracting *there*; consequently, C_{HL} raises *someone* to the outer specifier of T, forming (101).

(101) [$_{TP}$ someone [$_{T'}$ there [$_{T'}$ to be t(someone) in the room]]]

At a later stage in the derivation, C_{HL} reaches the following structure, whose head T requires a single specifier:

(102) [$_{TP}$ seems + T [$_{VP}$ t(seems) [$_{TP}$ someone [$_{T'}$ there [$_{T'}$ to be t(someone) in the room]]]]]

The next step fills the specifier of the matrix T to check the strong D-feature of the matrix T. In (102), *someone* is not in the minimal domain of CH the head of which is adjoined to the matrix T, and *someone* c-commands *there*; hence, *someone* is closer to the matrix T than *there*. Given this, the MLC prohibits the matrix T from attracting *there*; consequently, C_{HL} raises *someone* to the specifier of the matrix T, forming (103).

(103) [$_{TP}$ someone [$_{T'}$ seems + T [$_{VP}$ t(seems) [$_{TP}$ t'(someone) [$_{T'}$ there [$_{T'}$ to be t(someone) in the room]]]]]]

This derivation later yields an LF structure in which *there* in the inner specifier of the embedded T fails to c-command its associate *someone* in the specifier of the matrix T. The C-Command Condition prohibits *there* from attracting *someone*, and consequently, the D-feature of *there* survives intact to LF: the derivation yielding (103) fails to converge.

The fatal step was made in mapping (99) to (100). Suppose the second option is selected. Then, C_{HL} raises *someone* to the (inner) specifier of T, forming (104) (instead of (100)).

(104) [$_{TP}$ someone [$_{T'}$ to be t in the room]]

The next step fills the outer specifier of T to complete the checking of the strong D-feature of T. Given that T cannot attract *someone*, C_{HL} has no option but to insert the remaining expletive *there* in the outer specifier of T, forming (105).

(105) [$_{TP}$ there [$_{T'}$ someone [$_{T'}$ to be t(someone) in the room]]]

At a later stage in the derivation, C_{HL} reaches the following structure, whose head T requires a single specifier:

(106) [$_{TP}$ seems + T [$_{VP}$ t(seems) [$_{TP}$ there [$_{T'}$ someone [$_{T'}$ to be t(someone) in the room]]]]]

The next step fills the specifier of the matrix T to check the strong D-feature of the matrix T. In (106), *there* is not in the minimal domain of CH the head of which is adjoined to the matrix T, and *there* c-commands *someone*; hence, *there* is closer to the matrix T than *someone*. Given this, the MLC prohibits the matrix T from attracting *someone*; consequently, C_{HL} raises *there* to the specifier of the matrix T, forming (107).

(107) [$_{TP}$ there [$_{T'}$ seems + T [$_{VP}$ t(seems) [$_{TP}$ t(there) [$_{T'}$ someone [$_{T'}$ to be t(someone) in the room]]]]]]

In (107), *there* in the specifier of the matrix T c-commands its associate *someone* in the inner specifier of the embedded T; consequently, *there* can attract *someone*. In the LF component, C_{HL} adjoins the N-feature of *someone* to the D-feature of *there;* consequently, the D-feature of *there* undergoes erasure. The resulting LF structure satisfies all the morphological properties: the derivation yielding (107), unlike other derivations, converges. We have thus reached the following conclusion: for any derivation D associated with the initial numeration of (81b), D fails to converge if D inserts *there* in some position other than the outer specifier of T projecting two specifiers. That is, the insertion of *there* in the outer specifier of the embedded T of (81b) is required for convergence.[36]

To summarize, assuming that the Icelandic T, assigned the strong D-feature with an option to escape erasure when checked, can exercise this option at most once, I demonstrated that insertion of an expletive in the outer specifier of T projecting two specifiers is necessary for the derivations of (81a–b) to converge: insertion of an expletive in some position other than the outer specifier of T projecting two specifiers blocks convergence.

Chapter 3

Legitimate Steps and Movement Phenomena

The Minimalist Program, seeking a maximally simple design for language, explores a unified analysis of seemingly disparate movement phenomena. The task facing this approach is then to show that the apparent diversity of movement phenomena is illusory and epiphenomenal, resulting from the interaction of the principles of Universal Grammar (Chomsky 1994).

In this chapter, I examine a number of movement phenomena involving violations of *Relativized Minimality*, the *Superiority Condition*, and the *Proper Binding Condition*, and I argue that the various contrasts exhibited in these movement phenomena can be deduced from the computational principles that constrain syntactic application, in particular, the Minimal Link Condition (MLC), repeated in (1).

(1) *Minimal Link Condition*
H(K) attracts α only if there is no β, β closer to H(K) than α, such that H(K) attracts β.

Given (1), I demonstrate that the central cases motivating Relativized Minimality, the Superiority Condition, and the Proper Binding Condition each involve an illegitimate step (e.g., an application of Move violating the MLC).[1]

3.1 Deriving Relativized Minimality

3.1.1 Relativized Minimality
Rizzi (1990) provides a principled account of the following three seemingly distinct movement violations (Chomsky 1993):

(2) a. *$[_\alpha$ fix] John $[_\beta$ can] t(α) the car
b. *$[_\alpha$ John] seems $[_\beta$ it] is certain t(α) to be here
c. *$[_\alpha$ how] did John wonder $[_{CP}[_\beta$ what] Mary fixed t(β) t(α)]

(2a) violates the *Head Movement Constraint* (HMC). (2b) is a case of *superraising*. (2c) violates the *Wh-Island Constraint*. The deviance of (2a–c) is then deduced from the principle *Relativized Minimality*, stated in (3).[2]

(3) *Relativized Minimality*
α cannot cross (= move to a position c-commanding) β
if β c-commands α, and β is the same type as α.

The relevant types are characterized (or relativized) as (4a–c) (Chomsky and Lasnik 1993; Rizzi 1990).

(4) a. If α adjoins to a head, β is a head.
   b. If α moves to an A-position, β is an A-specifier.
   c. If α moves to an Ā-position, β is an Ā-specifier.

The relativized minimality analysis, incorporating the principle Relativized Minimality and the relevant types, captures the deviance of (2a–c) as follows. In (2a), the adjunction of α (*fix*) to the head C violates Relativized Minimality because it crosses the head β (*can*). In (2b), the movement of α (*John*) to the matrix A-position violates Relativized Minimality because it crosses the embedded A-specifier β (*it*). In (2c), the movement of α (*how*) to the matrix Ā-position violates Relativized Minimality because it crosses the embedded Ā-specifier β (*what*). Thus, (2a–c) each violate Relativized Minimality.

The relativized minimality analysis attains considerable descriptive adequacy, but as Chomsky and Lasnik (1993) point out, it lacks the generality that we would hope to find in an explanatory theory of language. More specifically, it incorporates both the head versus nonhead (bar level) distinction and the A versus Ā (positional) distinction.

3.1.2 Deriving the Central Cases Motivating Relativized Minimality

Under the Minimalist Program, the MLC excludes the derivations of (2a–c), and it does so without any reference to bar level or positional distinctions. Let us examine (2a–c) in turn.

First consider (2a). Suppose the C has a strong feature triggering subject-auxiliary inversion, and both *can* and *fix* can enter into a checking relation with a sublabel of the C.[3] Then, the MLC forces the C to attract the closest category, namely, *can*. Thus, the application of Move raising *fix* to the C in (2a) violates the MLC.[4] The deviance of (2b) is captured in the same way. Given that the matrix T has a strong feature triggering subject raising, the MLC forces the matrix T to attract the closest category that can enter into a checking relation with its sublabel, namely, *it*. Thus, the application of Move raising *John* to the specifier of the matrix T in (2b) violates the MLC. Finally, consider (2c). Given that the matrix C has a strong feature triggering *wh*-movement, the MLC forces the matrix C to attract the closest category that can enter into a checking relation with its sublabel, namely, *what*. Thus, the application of Move raising *how* to the specifier of the matrix C in (2c) violates the MLC.

Under the MLC analysis, therefore, the derivations of (2a–c), employing an illegitimate application of Move, induce deviance: the deviant (2a–c) receive a unified analysis in terms of the MLC.[5]

3.1.3 Conflicting C-Command Relations
Chomsky (1995, 304) notes that raising constructions such as (5) might pose a problem for the MLC analysis.

(5) [$_\alpha$ They] seem to [$_\beta$ him] [$_{TP}$ t(α) to like John].

In (5), *John* must be interpreted as disjoint from *him*. Chomsky takes such disjoint reference between *him* and *John* to be evidence that *him* c-commands into the embedded TP containing *John*. Given that *him* c-commands *John*, Condition C of the binding theory is violated if *him* takes *John* as its antecedent (Chomsky 1981). But then, *him* must also c-command *they* in the embedded TP (prior to the raising of *they*), which causes a problem for the attraction theory of movement (incorporating the MLC). Recall the definition of closeness, repeated in (6).

(6) β is closer to H(K) than α iff β c-commands α, and β is not in the minimal domain of CH, where CH is the chain headed by γ, and γ is adjoined to H(K).

Given (6), consider the following mapping:

(7) a. [$_{TP}$ T seem to [$_\beta$ him] [$_{TP}$ [$_\alpha$ they] to like John]]
   b. [$_{TP}$[$_\alpha$ they] [$_{T'}$ T seem to [$_\beta$ him] [$_{TP}$ t(α) to like John]]]

In (7a), *him* is not in the minimal domain of CH the head of which is adjoined to the matrix T, and *him* c-commands *they*; hence, *him* is closer to the matrix T than *they*. Given this, the MLC forces the matrix T to attract *him*. That is, contrary to fact, we expect that Move raising *they* in mapping (7a) to (7b) should count as an illegitimate application of Move (violating the MLC).

The problem, posed by (5), lies between the Condition C analysis and the MLC analysis: Condition C ensures the observed disjoint reference between *John* and *him* only if *him* c-commands into the embedded TP, but the MLC permits Move to raise *they* over *him* only if *him* does not c-command into the embedded TP.

To account for this apparent paradox, unlike Chomsky (1995), I assume that *him* does not c-command *they* in the embedded TP prior to the raising of *they*. First consider the "Larsonian shell" structure (8) (prior to the adjunction of *seem* to *v*) in which the verb *seem* has two internal arguments, PP and the embedded TP.

(8)

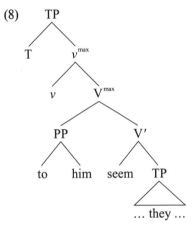

Assuming the standard definition of c-command (Reinhart 1976), in (8), the PP node dominates *him* but not the embedded TP. Hence, *him* does not c-command into the embedded TP (i.e., neither *him* nor *they* (in the embedded TP) c-commands the other: neither blocks the movement of the other). Thus, Move raising *they* over *him* to the specifier of the matrix T in mapping (7a) to (7b) counts as a legitimate application of Move, as desired.[6]

Let us turn to the fact that *John* must be interpreted as disjoint from *him* in (5). Suppose such disjoint reference is ensured by Condition C applying solely at LF (Chomsky 1993). Then, the derivation of (5) must yield an LF representation in which *him* or its referential property (or both) enter into a c-command relation with *John*. I propose that the covert feature movement of FF[him] plays a crucial role in generating such an LF representation of (5). That is, in the LF component, C_{HL} adjoins FF[him] to the preposition *to* for the checking of Case features of *him* and *to* ([−interpretable]), and this covert feature movement allows the referential property of *him* to enter into a c-command relation with *John*.

Suppose an r-expression must be interpreted as disjoint from every c-commanding phrase (Condition C). Then, *John* must be interpreted as disjoint from the PP (c-commanding *John*) (see the "Larsonian shell" structure (8)). Now notice that after the adjunction of FF[him] to the preposition *to*, the head of the PP (c-commanding *John*) contains FF[him] that includes the referential property of *him* (Chomsky 1995; Lasnik and Saito 1991).[7] In the resulting LF representation of (5), therefore, Condition C forces *John* to be interpreted as disjoint from this newly created PP whose head includes the referential property of *him*. In turn, this disjoint reference between *John* and the PP containing the referential property of *him* ensures the observed disjoint reference between *him* and *John* in (5).

Under this derivational analysis, *him* does not c-command *they* in the derivation of (5); hence, Move raising *they* over *him* counts as a legitimate application of Move. The fact that *John* must be interpreted as disjoint from *him* in (5) is ensured by Condition C applying to the LF representation of (5) resulting from the covert adjunction of FF[him] to the head of the PP (c-commanding *John*). Therefore, the seemingly paradoxical problem for the MLC analysis, posed by (5), receives a principled account without any special stipulation.[8]

3.2 Deriving the Superiority Condition

Chomsky (1993) suggests that under the minimalist approach, movement phenomena (e.g., relativized minimality and superiority phenomena) receive a unified analysis in terms of the notion "shortest move."[9] In this section, limiting discussion to the core cases motivating the Superiority Condition, I argue that the MLC derives not only Relativized Minimality but also the Superiority Condition: these two seemingly distinct movement phenomena receive a unified analysis in terms of the MLC.

3.2.1 The Superiority Condition

Chomsky (1973) discussed the following contrast, now known as the *standard superiority effect*:

(9) a. I wonder [$_{CP}$ who$_1$ [$_{TP}$ t$_1$ bought what$_2$]].
    b. *I wonder [$_{CP}$ what$_2$ [$_{TP}$ who$_1$ bought t$_2$]].

(9b) was excluded as a violation of the *Superiority Condition*, stated in (10).

(10) *Superiority Condition*
No rule can involve X, Y in the structure
… X … [… Z … WYV …] …
where the rule applies ambiguously to Z and Y, and Z is superior to Y.

The notion "superior" was defined as follows.

(11) The category A is taken to be superior to the category B if every major category dominating A dominates B as well but not conversely.

The superiority analysis, incorporating the Superiority Condition and the notion "superior," permits (9a) while excluding (9b). Given that *who* is superior to *what*, the Superiority Condition allows *who* to undergo *wh*-movement to the specifier of the embedded C while prohibiting *what* from undergoing *wh*-movement to the same position.

The superiority analysis further captures the following contrast, known as the *pure superiority effect* (Hendrick and Rochemont 1982; Pesetsky 1982, 1987):

(12) a.   Whom$_1$ did you persuade t$_1$ [to buy what$_2$]?
b.   ?*What$_2$ did you persuade whom$_1$ [to buy t$_2$]?

Given that *whom* is superior to *what*, the Superiority Condition allows *whom* to undergo *wh*-movement to the specifier of the matrix C while prohibiting *what* from undergoing *wh*-movement to the same position.[10,11]

3.2.2 Deriving the Core Cases Motivating the Superiority Condition

Under the Minimalist Program, these standard and pure superiority effects are deducible from the MLC.

First consider (9a–b). Given that the embedded C has a strong feature triggering *wh*-movement, the MLC forces it to attract the closest category that can enter into a checking relation with its sublabel, namely, *who*. Thus, the application of Move raising *who* to the specifier of the embedded C in (9a) satisfies the MLC, whereas the application of Move raising *what* to the specifier of the embedded C in (9b) violates it.

Now consider (12a–b). Given that the matrix C has a strong feature triggering *wh*-movement, the MLC forces it to attract the closest category that can enter into a checking relation with its sublabel, namely, *whom*.

Thus, the application of Move raising *whom* to the specifier of the matrix C in (12a) satisfies the MLC, whereas the application of Move raising *what* to the specifier of the matrix C in (12b) violates it.

Under the MLC analysis, therefore, the derivations of (9b) and (12b), just like the derivations of (2a–c), employing an illegitimate application of Move, induce deviance.[12]

3.2.3 Further Consequences

The MLC analysis of superiority effects further accounts for the absence of deviance in examples such as (13a) (Bošković 1993; Fiengo et al. 1988).

(13) a. I wonder [$_{CP}$ who$_2$ [$_{TP}$[pictures of who$_1$] pleased t_2]].
   b. *I wonder [$_{CP}$ who$_1$ [$_{TP}$[pictures of t_1] pleased who$_2$]].

Given that the embedded C has a strong feature triggering *wh*-movement, the MLC forces it to attract the closest category that can enter into a checking relation with its sublabel. Both *who$_1$* and *who$_2$* can qualify. That is, neither *who$_1$* nor *who$_2$* c-commands the other; hence, neither blocks the movement of the other. Thus, the application of Move raising *who$_2$* to the specifier of the embedded C in (13a) satisfies the MLC. Therefore, the derivation of (13a) induces no deviance. The application of Move raising *who$_1$* to the specifier of the embedded C in (13b) also satisfies the MLC, but violates the Subject Condition, repeated in (14) (see, among others, Chomsky 1973; Huang 1982; Lasnik and Saito 1984, 1992).[13]

(14) *Subject Condition*
   Extraction out of a subject is prohibited.

Therefore, the derivation of (13b) induces deviance because of a violation of the Subject Condition (but not a violation of the MLC).

Further, consider the absence of deviance in the following pairs:

(15) a. I wonder [$_{CP}$ what$_1$ [$_{TP}$ John hid t_1 where$_2$]].
   b. I wonder [$_{CP}$ where$_2$ [$_{TP}$ John hid what$_1$ t_2]].

(16) a. I wonder [$_{CP}$ what$_1$ [$_{TP}$ John hid t_1 when$_2$]].
   b. I wonder [$_{CP}$ when$_2$ [$_{TP}$ John hid what$_1$ t_2]].

To capture the absence of deviance in each of these pair, I adopt Huang's (1982) null preposition analysis. Huang points out that *where* and *when* (unlike *how* and *why*) can appear as a complement of a preposition (e.g., *from where* and *since when*). He further notes that *there* and *then* can be analyzed as pronominal forms of *where* and *when* (whereas no corresponding pronominal form exists for *how* and *why*). These facts lead him to propose that *where* and *when* are categories that can appear as a complement of a phonologically null preposition *p*, as shown in (17).[14]

(17) a. [$_{PP}$ *p* where]
     b. [$_{PP}$ *p* when]

Given Huang's null preposition analysis, I assume that in the derivations of (15a–b) and (16a–b), C_{HL} constructs the following structures in which PP asymmetrically c-commands the complement of the verb:

(18) a. [$_{CP}$[$_{TP}$ John [$_{vP}$ hid what [$_{PP}$ *p* where]]]]
     b. [$_{CP}$[$_{TP}$ John [$_{vP}$ hid what [$_{PP}$ *p* when]]]]

First consider the structure (18a) common to the derivations of (15a–b). Given that the C has a strong feature triggering *wh*-movement, the MLC forces it to attract the closest category that can enter into a checking relation with its sublabel. Both *what* and *where* can qualify. That is, under the null preposition analysis, neither *what* nor *where* c-commands the other; hence, neither blocks the movement of the other. Thus, both the application of Move raising *who* to the specifier of the C (in the derivation of (15a)) and the application of Move raising *where* to the specifier of the C (in the derivation of (15b)) satisfy the MLC.

Now consider the structure (18b) common to the derivations of (16a–b). Given that the C has a strong feature triggering *wh*-movement, the MLC forces it to attract the closest category that can enter into a checking relation with its sublabel. Both *what* and *when* can qualify. That is, under the null preposition analysis, neither *what* nor *when* c-commands the other; hence, neither blocks the movement of the other. Thus, both the application of Move raising *who* to the specifier of the C (in the derivation of (16a)) and the application of Move raising *when* to the specifier of the C (in the derivation of (16b)) satisfy the MLC.

As we have seen, under the Minimalist Program, relativized minimality phenomena and the core cases of superiority phenomena receive a unified analysis in terms of the MLC.[15]

3.3 Deriving the Proper Binding Condition

In this section, I show that the two central cases motivating the Proper Binding Condition can be explained: the one involving lowering is excluded by the C-Command Condition, and the one involving no lowering is excluded by the MLC.

3.3.1 The Proper Binding Condition

The contrast exhibited by pairs such as (19a–b) has been attributed to the presence of an unbound trace (see, among others, Fiengo 1977).

(19) a. I wonder [$_{CP}$ who$_1$ [$_{TP}$ Mary asked t_1
        [$_{CP}$ what$_2$ [$_{TP}$ John fixed t_2]]]].
     b. *I think [$_{CP}$ that [$_{TP}$ Mary asked t_1
        [$_{CP}$ who$_1$ [$_{TP}$ John fixed the car]]]].

Whereas t_1 and t_2 are each bound in (19a), t_1 is not in (19b). (19b) has been excluded by the *Proper Binding Condition* (PBC) (see, among others, Fiengo 1977; May 1977; Saito 1989, 1992).[16]

(20) *Proper Binding Condition*
     Traces must be bound.

Given that a trace is bound iff it is c-commanded by its antecedent, the PBC permits (19a) while excluding (19b). The PBC further captures the deviance of examples such as (21).

(21) *[$_{CP}$[Which picture of t_1]$_2$ do [$_{TP}$ you wonder
       [$_{CP}$ who$_1$ [$_{TP}$ John likes t_2]]]]?

In (21), the *wh*-movement of *who* to the specifier of the embedded C precedes the *wh*-movement of the embedded object *wh*-phrase (containing the trace of *who*) to the specifier of the matrix C. In the structure resulting from these two applications of *wh*-movement, t_2 is bound, but t_1 is not: the PBC is violated.

3.3.2 Deriving the Central Cases Motivating the Proper Binding Condition

Under the Minimalist Program, the derivation of (19b) is excluded by the C-Command Condition, repeated in (22).

(22) *C-Command Condition*
     H(K) attracts α only if H(K) c-commands α.

In (19b), the embedded C does not c-command the matrix object *who*; hence, the C-Command Condition prohibits it from attracting *who*. Thus, the derivation of (19b), employing an illegitimate application of Move, induces deviance. Under the C-Command Condition analysis, therefore, the deviance of cases such as (19b) (involving lowering) is captured without any reference to the PBC.[17]

Turning to the deviance of cases such as (21) (involving no lowering), let us consider the relevant aspects of the derivation of (21). Move first raises *who* to the specifier of the embedded C, then the embedded object *wh*-phrase (containing the trace of *who*) to the specifier of the matrix C, thereby inducing no violation of the C-Command Condition. To exclude the derivation of (21) (involving no lowering but inducing deviance), we need another principle.

Let us first ask whether the PBC can exclude the derivation of (21) under minimalist assumptions. The PBC was originally taken to be a condition applying at S-Structure. Such S-Structure application of the PBC would exclude the derivation of (21), which yields an S-Structure representation containing an unbound trace. But if we adopt the minimalist assumption that eliminates S-Structure (like D-Structure) as a level of representation (Chomsky 1993), there cannot be any conditions applying at S-Structure. Given this assumption, the PBC must be formulated as a condition applying at LF. But even such LF application of the PBC fails to exclude the LF structure of (21) if we adopt the *copy theory of movement* and the *Preference Principle* (Chomsky 1993).[18]

Given the copy theory of movement, C_{HL} generates the following structure for (21) to which Spell-Out applies:

(23) [$_{CP}$[which picture of t(who)] do you wonder
[$_{CP}$ who John likes t([which picture of t(who)])]]

Later, in the LF component, the Preference Principle (requiring a minimization of the restriction in the operator position, for example, specifier of C) converts (23) (roughly) to the following LF structure:

(24) [$_{CP}$ (which y) you wonder
[$_{CP}$ (which x) John likes (y picture of (x person))]]

In (24), the variables x and y are each bound; hence, LF application of the PBC is satisfied. Given the copy theory of movement and the Preference Principle, therefore, the LF application of the PBC cannot exclude the derivation of (21).

Instead of pursuing a PBC analysis any further, I would like to argue that the MLC analysis readily extends to capture the severe deviance of (21). I first point out that the derivation of (21) involves two illegitimate applications of Move. I then discuss an implication of such multiple violations.

Consider the relevant aspects of the derivation of (21). At some point in the derivation, C_{HL} constructs the following structure:

(25) [$_{CP}$[$_{TP}$ John likes [which picture of who]]]

Given that the C has a strong feature triggering *wh*-movement, the MLC forces it to attract the closest category that can enter into a checking relation with its sublabel, namely, *which*. Given that the raising of *which* alone causes the derivation to crash, C_{HL} can and should raise the minimal category containing *which* that allows convergence, namely, *which picture of who*. Thus, the application of Move raising *who* to the specifier of the C violates the MLC. Suppose C_{HL} employs this illegitimate application of Move. Then, C_{HL} yields (26).

(26) [$_{CP}$ who [$_{C'}$[$_{TP}$ John likes [which picture of t(who)]]]]

At a later stage in this derivation, C_{HL} reaches the following structure:

(27) [$_{CP}$ do [$_{TP}$ you wonder
[$_{CP}$ who [$_{C'}$[$_{TP}$ John likes [which picture of t(who)]]]]]]

Given that the matrix C has a strong feature triggering *wh*-movement, the MLC forces it to attract the closest category that can enter into a checking relation with its sublabel, namely, *who*. Thus, the application of Move raising *which picture of t(who)* to the specifier of the matrix C violates the MLC. Suppose C_{HL} employs this illegitimate application of Move. Then, C_{HL} yields (28).

(28) [$_{CP}$ [which picture of t(who)] [$_{C'}$ do [$_{CP}$ you wonder
[$_{CP}$ who [$_{C'}$[$_{TP}$ John likes t([which picture of t(who)])]]]]]]

As shown above, C_{HL} employs two illegitimate applications of Move to generate (28) (i.e., the structure of (21)), to which Spell-Out applies.

Now compare the severely deviant (21) with the marginally deviant (29). The derivations of (21) and (29) are associated with the same initial numeration, and they compete in the eyes of derivational economy.[19]

(29) ??[$_{CP}$ Who$_1$ do [$_{TP}$ you wonder
[$_{CP}$[which picture of t$_1$]$_2$ [$_{TP}$ John likes t$_2$]]]]?

Let us examine the relevant aspects of the derivation of (29). Notice that the structure (25) is common to the derivations of (21) and (29). In (25), the C has a strong feature triggering *wh*-movement; hence, the MLC forces it to attract the closest category that can enter into a checking relation with its sublabel, namely, *which*. Given that the raising of *which* alone causes the derivation to crash, C_{HL} can and should raise the minimal category containing *which* that allows convergence, namely, *which picture of who*. Thus, the application of Move raising *which picture of who* to the specifier of the C satisfies the MLC. Suppose C_{HL} employs this legitimate application of Move. Then, C_{HL} yields (30) (instead of (26)).

(30) [$_{CP}$[which picture of who]
    [$_{C'}$[$_{TP}$ John likes t([which picture of who])]]]

At a later stage in this derivation, C_{HL} reaches the following structure:

(31) [$_{CP}$ do [$_{CP}$ you wonder [$_{CP}$[which picture of who]
    [$_{C'}$[$_{TP}$ John likes t([which picture of who])]]]]]

Given that the matrix C has a strong feature triggering *wh*-movement, the MLC forces it to attract the closest category that can enter into a checking relation with its sublabel, namely, *which*. Given that the raising of *which* alone causes the derivation to crash, C_{HL} can and should raise the minimal category containing *which* that allows convergence, namely, *which picture of who*. Thus, the application of Move raising *who* to the specifier of the matrix C violates the MLC. Suppose C_{HL} employs this illegitimate application of Move. Then, C_{HL} yields (32).

(32) [$_{CP}$ who [$_{C'}$ do [$_{CP}$ you wonder [$_{CP}$[which picture of t(who)]
    [$_{C'}$[$_{TP}$ John likes t([which picture of who])]]]]]]

As shown above, C_{HL} employs only one illegitimate application of Move to generate (32) (i.e., the structure of (29)), to which Spell-Out applies.

Under the MLC analysis, the derivation of (21) employs two illegitimate applications of Move and induces severe deviance, whereas the derivation of (29) employs one illegitimate application of Move and induces marginal deviance. To explain why the derivation of (21) induces a greater degree of deviance than does the derivation of (29), I adopt the following (arguably natural) assumption (Chomsky 1965; Epstein 1990):[20]

(33) A derivation employing a greater number of illegitimate steps induces a greater degree of deviance.

Given (33), the derivation of (21) (employing two illegitimate applications of Move) exhibits a greater degree of deviance than does the derivation of (29) (employing one illegitimate application of Move).[21,22] Under the

MLC analysis (incorporating (33)), therefore, the severe deviance of cases such as (21) (involving no lowering) is captured without any reference to the PBC.

3.3.3 Further Consequences

The MLC analysis of PBC effects further captures the following contrast, the so-called nesting effect (Pesetsky 1982, 1987):

(34) a. ??What$_2$ did you wonder [$_{CP}$ whom$_1$ John persuaded t$_1$ to buy t$_2$]?
  b. ?*Whom$_1$ did you wonder [$_{CP}$ what$_2$ John persuaded t$_1$ to buy t$_2$]?

Pesetsky (1982, 1987) proposes a general condition on movement that captures this contrast. He calls it the *Nested Dependency Condition* (NDC).

(35) *Nested Dependency Condition*
  If two *wh*-trace dependencies overlap, one must contain the other.

Taking *wh*-trace dependencies to be LF chain structures formed by *wh*-movement, Pesetsky assigns the chain structures (36a–b) to (34a–b), respectively:

(36) a. what$_2$ whom$_1$ t$_1$ t$_2$

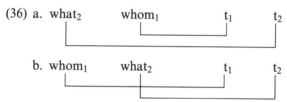

  b. whom$_1$ what$_2$ t$_1$ t$_2$

The LF structure of (34a) (assigned the nesting dependency (36a)) satisfies the NDC and the movement of *what* is therefore legitimate, whereas the LF structure of (34b) (assigned the intersecting dependency (36b)) violates the NDC and the movement of *whom* is therefore illegitimate.

This nesting effect follows rather straightforwardly from the MLC analysis: the derivation of (34a), involving one illegitimate application of Move, induces marginal deviance, whereas the derivation of (34b), involving two illegitimate applications of Move, induces severe deviance.

First consider the relevant aspects of the derivation of (34a). At some point in the derivation of (34a), C$_{HL}$ constructs the following structure:

(37) [$_{CP}$[$_{TP}$ John persuaded whom to buy what]]

Given that the C has a strong feature triggering *wh*-movement, the MLC forces it to attract the closest category that can enter into a checking relation with its sublabel, namely, *whom*. Thus, the application of Move raising *whom* to the specifier of the C satisfies the MLC. Suppose C_{HL} employs this legitimate application of Move. Then, C_{HL} yields (38).

(38) [$_{CP}$ whom [$_{C'}$[$_{TP}$ John persuaded t(whom) to buy what]]]

At a later stage in this derivation, C_{HL} reaches the following structure:

(39) [$_{CP}$ did [$_{TP}$ you wonder
      [$_{CP}$ whom [$_{C'}$[$_{TP}$ John persuaded t(whom) to buy what]]]]]

Given that the matrix C has a strong feature triggering *wh*-movement, the MLC forces it to attract the closest category that can enter into a checking relation with its sublabel, namely, *whom*. Thus, the application of Move raising *what* to the specifier of the matrix C violates the MLC. Suppose C_{HL} employs this illegitimate application of Move. Then, C_{HL} yields (40).

(40) [$_{CP}$ what [$_{C'}$ did [$_{TP}$ you wonder
      [$_{CP}$ whom [$_{C'}$[$_{TP}$ John persuaded t(whom) to buy t(what)]]]]]]

As shown above, C_{HL} employs only one illegitimate application of Move to generate (40) (i.e., the structure of (34a)), to which Spell-Out applies.

Now compare the derivation of the marginally deviant (34a) with the derivation of the severely deviant (34b). The derivations of (34a–b) are associated with the same initial numeration, and they compete in the eyes of derivational economy. Let us examine the relevant aspects of the derivation of (34b). Notice that the structure (37) is common to the derivations of (34a–b). In (37), the C has a strong feature triggering *wh*-movement; hence, the MLC forces it to attract the closest category that can enter into a checking relation with its sublabel, namely, *whom*. Thus, the application of Move raising *what* to the specifier of the C violates the MLC. Suppose C_{HL} employs this illegitimate application of Move. Then, C_{HL} yields (41) (instead of (38)).

(41) [$_{CP}$ what [$_{C'}$[$_{TP}$ John persuaded whom to buy t(what)]]]

At a later stage in this derivation, C_{HL} reaches the following structure:

(42) [$_{CP}$ did [$_{TP}$ you wonder
      [$_{CP}$ what [$_{C'}$[$_{TP}$ John persuaded whom to buy t(what)]]]]]

Given that the matrix C has a strong feature triggering *wh*-movement, the MLC forces it to attract the closest category that can enter into a checking relation with its sublabel, namely, *what*. Thus, the application of

Move raising *whom* to the specifier of the matrix C violates the MLC. Suppose C_{HL} employs this illegitimate application of Move. Then, C_{HL} yields (43).

(43) [$_{CP}$ whom [$_{C'}$ did [$_{TP}$ you wonder
   [$_{CP}$ what [$_{C'}$[$_{TP}$ John persuaded t(whom) to buy t(what)]]]]]]

As shown above, C_{HL} employs two illegitimate applications of Move to generate (43) (i.e., the structure of (34b)), to which Spell-Out applies.

Finally, recall (33), repeated here.

(33) A derivation employing a greater number of illegitimate steps induces a greater degree of deviance.

Given (33), the derivation of (34b) (employing two illegitimate applications of Move) exhibits a greater degree of deviance than does the derivation of (34a) (employing one illegitimate application of Move). Under the MLC analysis (incorporating (33)), therefore, the nesting effect is captured without any reference to the NDC.

The proposed analysis is further supported by the absence of deviance in examples such as (44) (see, among others, Huang 1993).

(44) I wonder [$_{CP}$[how certain [$_{TP}$ t$'_1$ to [$_{vP}$ t$_1$ win]]]$_2$ [$_{TP}$ John$_1$ is t$_2$]].

First recall Chomsky's (1995) version of the predicate-internal subject hypothesis (i.e., a subject is base-generated in the specifier of a light verb).[23] Given this, the trace of *John* occupying the specifier of the most deeply embedded T (namely, t$'_1$) becomes unbound when the embedded predicate is raised to the specifier of the embedded C; nevertheless, (44) exhibits no PBC effect.[24]

The MLC analysis correctly predicts that the derivation of (44) employs no illegitimate application of Move and converges. Consider the relevant aspects of the derivation of (44). At some point in the derivation of (44), C_{HL} constructs the following structure (in which *John* has been raised to the specifier of the most deeply embedded T):

(45) [$_{TP}$ is [$_\alpha$ how certain [$_{TP}$ John to [$_{vP}$ t(John) win]]]]

Given that the higher T has a strong feature triggering subject raising, the MLC forces it to attract the closest category that can enter into a checking relation with its sublabel, namely, *John*. Thus, the application of Move raising *John* to the specifier of the higher T satisfies the MLC. Suppose C_{HL} employs this legitimate application of Move. Then, C_{HL} yields (46).

(46) [$_{TP}$ John [$_{T'}$ is [$_{α}$ how certain [$_{TP}$ t'(John) to [$_{vP}$ t(John) win]]]]]

At a later stage in this derivation, C_{HL} reaches the following structure:

(47) [$_{CP}$[$_{TP}$ John [$_{T'}$ is [$_{α}$ how certain [$_{TP}$ t'(John) to [$_{vP}$ t(John) win]]]]]]

Given that the C has a strong feature triggering *wh*-movement, the MLC forces it to attract the closest category that can enter into a checking relation with its sublabel, namely, *how*. Given that the raising of *how* alone causes the derivation to crash, C_{HL} can and should raise the minimal category containing *how* that allows convergence, namely, α containing the traces of *John*. Thus, the application of Move raising α to the specifier of the C satisfies the MLC. Suppose C_{HL} employs this legitimate application of Move. Then, C_{HL} yields (48).

(48) [$_{CP}$[$_{α}$ how certain [$_{TP}$ t'(John) to [$_{vP}$ t(John) win]]]
      [$_{C'}$[$_{TP}$ John [$_{T'}$ is t(α)]]]]

This derivation later yields (49).

(49) [$_{CP}$[$_{TP}$ I wonder [$_{CP}$[$_{α}$ how certain [$_{TP}$ t'(John) to [$_{vP}$ t(John) win]]]
      [$_{C'}$[$_{TP}$ John [$_{T'}$ is t(α)]]]]]]

As shown above, C_{HL} employs no illegitimate application of Move to generate (49) (i.e., the structure of (44)), to which Spell-Out applies. In the LF component, the Preference Principle converts (49) (roughly) to the following structure:

(50) [$_{CP}$[$_{TP}$ I wonder [$_{CP}$ (how *x*) [$_{TP}$ John is
      (*x* certain [$_{TP}$ t'(John) to [$_{vP}$ t(John) win])]]]]]

Assuming that the LF representation of (44), given in (50) (in which the variable *x* and the traces of *John* are each bound), is legitimate, the derivation of (44) converges: the MLC analysis captures, without special stipulation, the absence of a PBC effect in (44).

3.4 Summary

In this chapter, I demonstrated that under the Minimalist Program, a number of seemingly disparate syntactic phenomena motivating Relativized Minimality, the Superiority Condition, and the PBC receive a unified analysis. I showed that the various contrasts exhibited in these (and related) movement phenomena can be deduced from the MLC with its supplementary (but arguably natural) assumption (33).

3.5 Appendix: Scrambling and Unbound Traces

In this appendix, I examine cases involving unbound traces formed by other types of movement such as *short scrambling, long scrambling,* and *topicalization.* I demonstrate that the MLC analysis captures various contrasts in these cases if such instances of movement are understood to be morphologically driven as well. The appendix consists of two subsections: subsection 3.5.1 examines German data involving short scrambling and topicalization, and subsection 3.5.2 examines Japanese data involving long scrambling.

3.5.1 German

In German, an infinitival clause from which some element has undergone short scrambling cannot undergo short scrambling, but it can undergo topicalization (see, among others, Den Besten and Webelhuth 1990; Müller 1993, 1994; Müller and Sternefeld 1993; Grewendorf and Sabel 1994). Consider the following contrast:

(51) *daß [t_1 zu lesen]$_2$ keiner [das Buch]$_1$ t_2 versucht hat
　　　 that　to read　no-one the book　　　 tried　 has
　　　 'that no one has tried to read the book'

　　a. *Short scrambling*
　　　 daß keiner [das Buch]$_1$ [t_1 zu lesen]$_2$ versucht hat
　　　 that no-one the book　　　 to read　 tried　 has

　　b. *Short scrambling*
　　　 daß [t_1 zu lesen]$_2$ keiner [das Buch]$_1$ t_2 versucht hat
　　　 that　to read　no-one the book　　　 tried　 has

(52) [t_1 zu lesen]$_2$ hat keiner [das Buch]$_1$ t_2 versucht
　　　 to read　 has no-one the book　　　 tried
　　　 'No one has tried to read the book.'

　　a. *Short scrambling*
　　　 hat keiner [das Buch]$_1$ [t_1 zu lesen]$_2$ versucht
　　　 has no-one the book　　　 to read　 tried

　　b. *Topicalization*
　　　 [t_1 zu lesen]$_2$ hat keiner [das Buch]$_1$ t_2 versucht
　　　 to read　 has no-one the book　　　 tried

In (51), the short scrambling of the embedded object *das Buch* 'the book' (see (51a)) precedes the short scrambling of the infinitival clause (containing the trace of the scrambled object) (see (51b)), rendering the trace of the scrambled object unbound. The derivation of (51) induces deviance. In (52), the short scrambling of the embedded object *das Buch* 'the book' (see (52a)) precedes the topicalization of the infinitival clause (containing the trace of the scrambled object) (see (52b)), rendering the trace of the scrambled object unbound. The derivation of (52), unlike the derivation of (51), induces no deviance.

To capture the contrast between (51) and (52), Müller (1993, 1994) presents the following generalization:[25]

(53) X cannot undergo α-movement resulting in a structure in which X dominates an unbound trace of Y, if the antecedent of Y has also undergone α-movement.

Assuming that short scrambling is A-movement, and topicalization is $\bar{\text{A}}$-movement, Müller demonstrates that the derivation of (51) violates (53), whereas the derivation of (52) does not. In the derivation of (51), the short scrambling (A-movement) of the embedded object precedes the short scrambling (A-movement) of the infinitival clause, rendering the trace of the scrambled object unbound; hence, the derivation of (51) violates (53). In the derivation of (52), however, the short scrambling (A-movement) of the embedded object precedes the topicalization ($\bar{\text{A}}$-movement) of the infinitival clause, rendering the trace of the scrambled object unbound; hence, the derivation of (52) does not violate (53). The contrast between (51) and (52) thus follows from Müller's generalization.

The MLC analysis, motivated on independent grounds, captures Müller's generalization if short scrambling and topicalization are driven by the checking of a strong "argument" feature and a strong "operator" feature, respectively.[26]

Let us first examine the relevant aspects of the derivation of (51). At some point in the derivation, C_{HL} constructs the following structure, in which the infinitival clause α contains the embedded object β:

(54) ... [$_α$[$_β$ das Buch] zu lesen] ...

In (54), both α and β can check a strong feature triggering short scrambling. At a later stage in the derivation, C_{HL} introduces into the tree a category bearing a strong feature triggering short scrambling. Given this, the MLC forces it to attract the closest category that can enter into a checking relation with its sublabel, namely, the head H(α) of α (which is closer to this attracting category than β). Given that the raising of H(α) alone causes the derivation to crash, C_{HL} can and should raise the minimal category containing H(α) that allows convergence, namely, α. Thus, the application of Move raising β (to check the strong feature triggering short scrambling) violates the MLC. Suppose C_{HL} employs this illegitimate application of Move. Then, C_{HL} yields (55).

(55) $[_\beta$ das Buch] ... $[_\alpha$ t(β) zu lesen] ...

Later, C_{HL} introduces into the tree another category bearing a strong feature triggering short scrambling. Given this, the MLC forces it to attract the closest category that can enter into a checking relation with its sublabel, namely, β.[27] Thus, the application of Move raising α (to check the strong feature triggering short scrambling) violates the MLC. Suppose C_{HL} employs this illegitimate application of Move. Then, C_{HL} yields (56).

(56) $[_\alpha$ t(β) zu lesen] ... $[_\beta$ das Buch] ... t(α) ...

This derivation yields the structure of (51) to which Spell-Out applies, fully represented as (57) (with glosses).

(57) daß $[_\alpha$ t(β) zu lesen] keiner $[_\beta$ das Buch] t(α) versucht hat
    that   to read no-one the book   tried   has

As shown above, the derivation of (51) employs two illegitimate applications of Move to yield (57), thereby inducing severe deviance.[28]

Now let us examine the relevant aspects of the derivation of (52). At some point in the derivation of (52), C_{HL} constructs the following structure, in which the infinitival clause α contains the embedded object β:

(58) ... $[_\alpha$ $[_\beta$ das Buch] zu lesen] ...

In (58), α can check a strong feature triggering topicalization, whereas β can check a strong feature triggering short scrambling. At a later stage in the derivation, C_{HL} introduces into the tree a category bearing a strong feature triggering short scrambling. Given this, the MLC forces it to attract the closest category that can enter into a checking relation with its sublabel, namely, β.[29] Thus, the application of Move raising β (to check the strong feature triggering short scrambling) satisfies the MLC. Suppose C_{HL} employs this legitimate application of Move. Then, C_{HL} yields (59).

(59) $[_\beta$ das Buch] ... $[_\alpha$ t(β) zu lesen] ...

Later, C_{HL} introduces into the tree a category bearing a strong feature triggering topicalization. Given this, the MLC forces it to attract the closest category that can enter into a checking relation with its sublabel, namely, α.[30] Thus, the application of Move raising α (to check the strong feature triggering topicalization) satisfies the MLC. Suppose C_{HL} employs this legitimate application of Move. Then, C_{HL} yields (60).

(60) [α t(β) zu lesen] ... [β das Buch] ... t(α) ...

This derivation yields the structure of (52) to which Spell-Out applies, fully represented as (61) (with glosses).

(61) [α t(β) zu lesen] hat keiner [β das Buch] t(α) versucht
          to read   has no-one   the book   tried

As shown above, the derivation of (52) employs no illegitimate applica-tion of Move to yield (61), thereby inducing no deviance.[31]

In this subsection, I demonstrated that the MLC analysis captures Müller's generalization (e.g., the contrast between (51) and (52)) if short scrambling and topicalization are instances of movement driven by mor-phological necessity.

3.5.2 Japanese

One of the central cases motivating S-Structure application of the PBC is drawn from Japanese and involves two instances of long scrambling (see, among others, Haig 1976; Harada 1977; Saito 1985, 1989, 1992).[32] First consider the following mapping:

(62) a. John-ga   [CP Mary-ga   [sono hon-o]₁   yonda-to] itta (koto)
          John-NOM   Mary-NOM   that book-ACC read-COMP said (fact)
          'John said that Mary read that book.'

    b. [sono hon-o]₁   John-ga   [CP Mary-ga   t₁ yonda-to] itta (koto)
          that book-ACC John-NOM   Mary-NOM   read-COMP said (fact)

In the mapping from (62a) to (62b), the embedded object *sono hon-o* 'that book' is scrambled out of the embedded CP to the sentence-initial posi-tion. Call this scrambling (which crosses a clause boundary) *long scram-bling*. The categories undergoing long scrambling also include CP, as shown in the following mapping:

(63) a. Bill-ga   [CP John-ga   [CP Mary-ga   sono hon-o   yonda-to]₁
          Bill-NOM   John-NOM   Mary-NOM   that book-ACC read-COMP
          itta-to]   omotteiru (koto)
          said-COMP think   (fact)
          'Bill thinks that John said that Mary read that book.'

    b. [CP Mary-ga   sono hon-o   yonda-to]₁ Bill-ga   [CP John-ga
          Mary-NOM   that book-ACC read-COMP   Bill-NOM   John-NOM
          t₁ itta-to]   omotteiru (koto)
          said-COMP think   (fact)

In the mapping from (63a) to (63b), the most deeply embedded CP is scrambled out of the embedded CP to the sentence-initial position. Now consider the following example involving two instances of long scrambling, one of the central cases motivating S-Structure application of the PBC (Saito 1989, 1992):

(64)   *[CP Mary-ga   t₁ yonda-to]₂ Bill-ga   [sono hon-o]₁   John-ga
        Mary-NOM   read-COMP Bill-NOM that book-ACC John-NOM
        t₂ itta-to   omotteiru (koto)
        said-COMP think   (fact)
        'Bill thinks that John said that Mary read that book.'
   a. *Long scrambling*
        Bill-ga   [sono hon-o]₁   John-ga   [CP Mary-ga   t₁ yonda-to]₂
        Bill-NOM   that book-ACC John-NOM   Mary-NOM   read-COMP
        itta-to   omotteiru (koto)
        read-COMP think   (fact)
   b. *Long scrambling*
        [CP Mary-ga   t₁ yonda-to]₂ Bill-ga   [sono hon-o]₁   John-ga
        Mary-NOM   read-COMP Bill-NOM that book-ACC John-NOM
        t₂ itta-to   omotteiru (koto)
        said-COMP think   (fact)

In (64), the long scrambling of the embedded object *sono hon-o* 'that book' (see (64a)) precedes the long scrambling of the most deeply embedded CP (containing the trace of the scrambled object) (see (64b)), rendering the trace of the scrambled object unbound. Given that the material undergoing long scrambling can be reconstructed (or undone) in the LF component, Saito (1989, 1992) excludes (64) by appealing to S-Structure application of the PBC.[33]

The MLC analysis captures the severe deviance of (64) if long scrambling is driven by the checking of a strong "operator" feature.

Let us examine the relevant aspects of the derivation of (64). At some point in the derivation of (64), C_{HL} constructs the following structure, in which the most deeply embedded clause α contains the embedded object β:

(65) ... [α Mary-ga [β sono hon-o] yonda-to] ...

In (65), both α and β can check a strong feature triggering long scrambling. At a later stage in the derivation, C_{HL} introduces into the tree a category bearing a strong feature triggering long scrambling. Given this, the MLC forces it to attract the closest category that can enter into a checking relation with its sublabel, namely, the head $H(\alpha)$ of α (which is closer to this attracting category than β). Given that the raising of $H(\alpha)$ alone causes the derivation to crash, C_{HL} can and should raise the minimal category containing $H(\alpha)$ that allows convergence, namely, α. Thus, the application of Move raising β (to check the strong feature triggering long scrambling) violates the MLC. Suppose C_{HL} employs this illegitimate application of Move. Then, C_{HL} yields (66).

(66) $[_\beta$ sono hon-o] ... $[_\alpha$ Mary-ga t(β) yonda-to] ...

Later, C_{HL} introduces into the tree another category bearing a strong feature triggering long scrambling. Given this, the MLC forces it to attract the closest category that can enter into a checking relation with its sublabel, namely, β.[34] Thus, the application of Move raising α (to check the strong feature triggering long scrambling) violates the MLC. Suppose C_{HL} employs this illegitimate application of Move. Then, C_{HL} yields (67).

(67) $[_\alpha$ Mary-ga t(β) yonda-to] ... $[_\beta$ sono hon-o] ... t(α) ...

This derivation yields the structure of (64) to which Spell-Out applies, fully represented as (68) (with glosses).

(68) $[_\alpha$ Mary-ga   t(β) yonda-to] Bill-ga $[_\beta$ sono hon-o]   John-ga
      Mary-NOM   read-COMP Bill-NOM   that book-ACC John-NOM
      t(α) itta-to   omotteiru (koto)
      said-COMP think   (fact)

As shown above, the derivation of (64) employs two illegitimate applications of Move to yield (68), thereby inducing severe deviance.[35]

In this subsection, I demonstrated that the MLC analysis captures the deviance of (64) (motivating the S-Structure application of the PBC) if long scrambling is an instance of movement driven by morphological necessity.

Chapter 4

Chain Formation and Degrees of Deviance

In the preceding chapter, I argued that the increased deviance of derivations involving two illegitimate applications of Move is determined in terms of the number of such illegitimate steps: a derivation employing a greater number of illegitimate steps induces a greater degree of deviance.

In this chapter, I examine other types of derivations that employ only one illegitimate application of Move but vary in their degree of deviance (e.g., *wh*-island violations involving adjuncts are far more severe than *wh*-island violations involving arguments). I argue that degrees of deviance exhibited by such derivations are determined in terms of *LF legitimacy*. A derivation employing one illegitimate step but yielding an LF representation satisfying the condition of *Full Interpretation* (FI) is only marginally deviant. By contrast, a derivation similarly employing one illegitimate step but yielding an LF representation violating FI is, naturally, more severely deviant.

4.1 Degrees of Deviance: A Problem

As is well known, *wh*-island violations such as (1a) involving adjuncts are far more severe than *wh*-island violations such as (1b) involving arguments.[1]

(1) a. *How₁ do you wonder [CP whether John fixed the car t₁]?
    b. ??What₁ do you wonder [CP whether John fixed t₁]?

First consider the derivation of (1a). Given that the matrix C has a strong feature triggering *wh*-movement, the MLC forces it to attract the closest category that can enter into a checking relation with its sublabel, namely, *whether*.[2] Thus, the application of Move raising *how* to the specifier of the matrix C violates the MLC. Now consider the derivation of (1b). Given that the matrix C has a strong feature triggering *wh*-movement, the MLC forces it to attract the closest category that can enter into a checking relation with its sublabel, namely, *whether.* Thus, the application of Move raising *what* to the specifier of the matrix C violates the MLC.

Given that the derivations of (1a–b) each employ only one illegitimate application of Move (violating the MLC), the contrast in (1) poses a problem for the analysis of degrees of deviance. Recall that this analysis incorporates the following assumption: a derivation employing a greater number of illegitimate steps induces a greater degree of deviance (see section 3.3). Now suppose a single violation of the MLC yields marginal deviance. Then, the MLC analysis predicts that (1a–b) each exhibit the same degree of deviance (i.e., marginal deviance), contrary to fact.[3] In minimalist terms, the contrast in (1) is stated as follows:

(2) An MLC violation involving adjuncts is far more severe than an
    MLC violation involving arguments.

Let us elaborate the statement (2). Consider the following contrast, which shows that the degree of deviance varies even among *wh*-island violations involving arguments:

(3) a.   *What$_1$ do you wonder [$_{CP}$ whether t$_1'$ was fixed t$_1$]?
    b.   ??What$_1$ do you wonder [$_{CP}$ whether John fixed t$_1$]?

Like the derivations of (1a–b), the derivations of (3a–b) employ only one illegitimate application of Move (violating the MLC).

First consider the derivation of (3a). At some point in the derivation, C$_{HL}$ employs an application of Move raising *what* from the embedded object position to the specifier of the embedded T, which satisfies the MLC. At a later stage in the derivation, C$_{HL}$ employs an application of Move raising *what* from the embedded subject position to the specifier of the matrix C, which violates the MLC. Now consider the derivation of (3b). At some point in the derivation, C$_{HL}$ employs an application of Move raising *what* from the embedded object position to the specifier of the matrix C, which violates the MLC.

Therefore, the derivations of (3a–b) employ only one illegitimate application of Move (involving an argument) but vary in their degree of deviance. To capture the contrast in (3) (in addition to the contrast in (1)), let us modify (2) as follows:

(4) An MLC violation involving adjuncts or subjects is far more severe
    than an MLC violation involving verbal complements.

Let us further elaborate this statement. Consider the following contrast (Rizzi 1990):

(5) a. *How many pounds$_1$ do you wonder
        [$_{CP}$ whether John weighed t$_1$]?
    b. ??What$_1$ do you wonder
        [$_{CP}$ whether John weighed t$_1$]?

Suppose the verb *weigh* can take as its complement either a "measure" object (e.g., *how many pounds*), which I will call a *quasi object*, or a "patient" object (e.g., *what*), which I will call an *object*. Then, (5) shows that the degree of deviance varies even among *wh*-violations involving verbal complements: quasi objects and objects.[4,5] Now notice that the derivations of (5a–b) employ only one illegitimate application of Move (violating the MLC).

First consider the derivation of (5a). At some point in the derivation, C_{HL} employs an application of Move raising the quasi object *how many pounds* to the specifier of the matrix C, which violates the MLC. Now consider the derivation of (5b). At some point in the derivation, C_{HL} employs an application of Move raising the object *what* to the specifier of the matrix C, which violates the MLC.

Therefore, the derivations of (5a–b) employ only one illegitimate application of Move (involving a verbal complement) but vary in their degree of deviance. We thus modify (4) as follows:

(6) An MLC violation involving adjuncts, subjects, or quasi objects is
     far more severe than an MLC violation involving objects.

This statement captures the contrasts in pairs such as (1a–b), (3a–b), and (5a–b), but it remains a description of the observed degrees of deviance, resisting any explanation in terms of the number of illegitimate steps. Notice that all the derivations examined here employ only one illegitimate application of Move (violating the MLC).

In what follows, I argue that the observed degrees of deviance (exhibited by (1a–b), (3a–b), and (5a–b)) are determined in terms of *LF legitimacy*. A derivation employing only one illegitimate application of Move but inducing severe deviance yields an illegitimate LF representation (containing an illegitimate object); hence, it crashes because of a violation of FI at LF. By contrast, a derivation employing only one illegitimate application of Move but inducing marginal deviance yields a legitimate LF representation (containing no illegitimate object); hence, it converges with marginal deviance as a result of employing one illegitimate step.

4.2   LF Objects and the Chain Formation Algorithm

In this section, I first review what counts as a legitimate object at LF. I then formulate a general chain formation algorithm (generating LF objects).

Chomsky (1993) takes economy of representation to be nothing other than FI: every object at the interface must receive an "external" interpretation. To be interpreted by the external systems—namely, the articulatory-perceptual (A-P) system and the conceptual-intentional (C-I) system—each representation must consist of legitimate objects at the interface. Given this, we say that a derivation D with a pair (π, λ) converges if π and λ satisfy FI at PF and at LF, respectively; otherwise, D crashes. Thus, FI is a condition on convergence: it determines the set of convergent derivations.

Under the Minimalist Program, PF is a representation consisting of universal phonetics, whereas LF is a representation consisting of chains. Such chains are taken to be pairs of distinct positions formed by the operation Move (Chomsky 1995, 252). To be concrete, let us (tentatively) assume the following algorithm:

(7) Move raising (a feature of) α from a position P_1 to a position P_2 forms a chain consisting of P_1 and P_2.

The LF chains (formed by the algorithm (7)) that concern us here include argument chains, adjunct chains, and operator-variable chains, defined as (8a–c) (see, among others, Browning 1987; Chomsky 1981, 1991, 1993; Chomsky and Lasnik 1993).[6]

(8) a. An argument chain is headed by an element in a Case-checking position and terminates with an element in a θ-marked position.
      b. An adjunct chain is headed by and terminates with an element in a non-L-related position(s).
      c. An operator-variable chain is headed by an element in a non-L-related position and terminates with an element in a Case-checking position.

The notion "(non-)L-related" is defined as (9) (Chomsky 1993; Chomsky and Lasnik 1993; Mahajan 1990).

(9) A position is L-related if it is in a checking configuration with a head containing a lexical feature (e.g., a V-feature); otherwise, it is non-L-related.

Examples such as (10) support the claim that an argument chain (headed by an argument) must be a nontrivial chain terminating with an element in a θ-marked position (see (8a)).

(10) *Mary seems that John fixed the car.

In (10), the argument *Mary* constitutes a single-membered chain lacking an associated θ-marked position. That is, the derivation of (10) yields an LF representation inducing a violation of the *θ-Criterion*, which I take to be part of FI at LF; hence, the derivation of (10) crashes (see Chomsky 1981, 1994, 1995). Similarly, examples such as (11) support the claim that an operator-variable chain (headed by an operator) must be a nontrivial chain terminating with an element in a Case-checking position (see (8c)).

(11) *What did John fix the car?

In (11), the operator *what* constitutes a single-membered chain lacking an associated Case-checking position. That is, the derivation of (11) yields an LF representation inducing a violation of the ban on *vacuous quantification*, which I take to be part of FI at LF; hence, the derivation of (11) crashes (see Chomsky 1982, 1986a,b, 1991, 1995; Chomsky and Lasnik 1993). Given that the failure of convergence induces severe deviance, these nonconvergent derivations of (10) and (11) induce severe deviance, as desired.

Returning to the three legitimate LF chains (defined as (8a–c)), consider the following chains formed in the derivations of (12a–c):

(12) a. $[_{CP}[_{TP} [_\alpha$ the car] was fixed $t(\alpha)]]$
   b. $[_{CP}[_\alpha$ how] did $[_{TP}$ John fix $+ v$ the car $t(\alpha)]]$
   c. $[_{CP}[_\alpha$ what] $[_{TP} t'(\alpha)$ was fixed $t(\alpha)]]$

In the derivation of (12a), Move raises α to the specifier of T, forming an argument chain CH $(\alpha, t(\alpha))$. In the derivation of (12b), Move raises α to the specifier of C, forming an adjunct chain CH $(\alpha, t(\alpha))$. In the derivation of (12c), Move raises α to the specifier of T; later, it raises α to the specifier of C. The former application of Move forms an argument chain CH $(t'(\alpha), t(\alpha))$; the latter application of Move forms an operator-variable chain CH $(\alpha, t'(\alpha))$. In each derivation, a single application of Move operates over two positions, and a resulting chain occupies these two positions.

However, this analysis faces the following problem. Compare the argument chain CH $(\alpha, t(\alpha))$ in (12a) with the argument chain CH $(\alpha, t(\alpha))$ in (13), formed by successive applications of Move.

(13) [$_{CP}$[$_{TP}$[$_\alpha$ the car] seemed [$_{TP}$ t'(α) to be fixed t(α)]]]

In the derivation of (13), Move raises α to the specifier of the embedded T; later, it raises α to the specifier of the matrix T. The pair (t'(α), t(α)) results from the former application of Move, whereas the pair (α, t'(α)) results from the latter application of Move. Given that an argument chain is headed by an element in a Case-checking position and terminates with an element in a θ-marked position (see (8a)), neither the pair (t'(α), t(α)) nor the pair (α, t'(α)) is an argument chain: the head of the former pair occupies a non-Case-checking position, whereas the tail of the latter pair occupies a non-θ-marked position. What counts as an argument chain (defined as (8a)) is the pair (α, t(α)) headed by α in the Case-checking position and terminating with t(α) in the θ-marked position (Chomsky 1995, 300). Notice here that no single application of Move in the derivation of (13) operates over the two positions occupied by the argument chain CH (α, t(α)).

This problem suggests that an application of Move raising (a feature of) α from a position P_1 to a position P_2 can form a chain other than the one consisting of the departure site P_1 and the landing site P_2. Following this guiding idea, I replace (7) with the following chain formation algorithm:

(14) Move raising (a feature of) α to a position P can form ≥ 1 chain(s) consisting of P and any other position associated with (a feature of) α.

Given (14), the latter application of Move raising α to the specifier of the matrix T in the derivation of (13) can form the argument chain CH (α, t(α)), headed by α in the Case-checking position and terminating with t(α) in the θ-marked position. That is, the analysis incorporating (14) (henceforth, the chain formation analysis), unlike previous analyses taking a chain to be a history of movement, permits a single application of Move raising α to form ≥ 1 chain(s) occupying the landing site of α and any other position associated with (a feature of) α.

The chain formation analysis is further supported by the formation of operator-variable chains such as CH (α, FF[α]) in (15).

(15) [$_{CP}$[$_\alpha$ what] did [$_{TP}$ John FF[α] + [fix + v] t(α)]]

In the derivation of (15), Move overtly raises α to the specifier of C; later, it covertly adjoins FF[α] to the complex head *fix* + v to check the Case features of α and *fix*. Recall that Case features are [−interpretable]; hence, they must be checked and erased before LF.

Now notice that, in the derivation of (15), the overt application of Move raising α does not form an operator-variable chain. Given that an operator-variable chain terminates with an element in a Case-checking position (see (8c)), the pair $(\alpha, t(\alpha))$ formed by the overt application of Move raising α is not an operator-variable chain since the position occupied by $t(\alpha)$ is not a Case-checking position. What counts as an operator-variable chain (defined as (8c)) is the pair $(\alpha, FF[\alpha])$ terminating with $FF[\alpha]$ in a Case-checking position. Then, a question arises about which application of Move forms the operator-variable chain CH $(\alpha, FF[\alpha])$ in the derivation of (15).

Under the chain formation analysis, the LF application of Move adjoining $FF[\alpha]$ to the complex head *fix* $+ v$ forms not only the argument chain CH $(FF[\alpha], t[\alpha])$ headed by $FF[\alpha]$ in a Case-checking position and terminating with $t(\alpha)$ in a θ-marked position, but also the operator-variable chain CH $(\alpha, FF[\alpha])$ headed by α in a non-L-related position and terminating with $FF[\alpha]$ in a Case-checking position.[7] Recall that the chain formation analysis permits a single application of Move raising $FF[\alpha]$ to form ≥ 1 chain(s) consisting of $FF[\alpha]$ and any other position associated with (a feature of) α, namely, the argument chain CH $(FF[\alpha], t(\alpha))$ and the operator-variable chain CH $(\alpha, FF[\alpha])$.

In this section, I argued that the chain formation algorithm given in (14) is essentially motivated to generate LF chains (see (8a–c)), including argument chains such as CH $(\alpha, t(\alpha))$ in (13) and operator-variable chains such as CH $(\alpha, FF[\alpha])$ in (15).

4.3 The Chain Formation Condition: A Proposal

In this section, I first propose a general condition on the chain formation algorithm. I then demonstrate that the greater degree of deviance exhibited by (1a), (3a), and (5a) (and other related cases) results from the failure of convergence because of a violation of FI at LF.

4.3.1 Argument versus Adjunct

Adopting the chain formation analysis, let us examine the severe deviance of (1a), repeated in (16).

(16) *How$_1$ do you wonder [$_{CP}$ whether John fixed the car t$_1$]?

Recall that the derivation of (16) involves one illegitimate application of Move (violating the MLC). Consider the following mapping:

(17) a. [$_{CP}$ do [$_{TP}$ you wonder + v
        [$_{CP}$ whether [$_{TP}$ John fixed + v the car [$_\alpha$ how]]]]]
     b. [$_{CP}$[$_\alpha$ how] [$_{C'}$ do [$_{TP}$ you wonder + v
        [$_{CP}$ whether [$_{TP}$ John fixed + v the car t(α)]]]]]

In mapping (17a) to (17b), C_{HL} employs an application of Move raising α to the specifier of the matrix C, which violates the MLC. Given that a single violation of the MLC yields only marginal deviance, we expect that there is some additional violation contributing to the severe deviance of (16).

Following this guiding idea, I propose that the derivation of (16), involving the illegitimate step (in mapping (17a) to (17b)), necessarily induces a violation of FI at LF. More specifically, I incorporate the following (arguably natural) condition on the chain formation algorithm, which we may call the *Chain Formation Condition* (CFC):

(18) *Chain Formation Condition*
     An application of Move forms ≥ 1 chain(s) only if it is legitimate
     (= violation-free).

Given the CFC, an application of Move violating the MLC forms no chain. So, for example, the *wh*-island extraction that takes place in mapping (17a) to (17b) (which raises a *wh*-phrase out of a *wh*-island, thereby inducing a violation of the MLC) forms no chain consisting of the moved *wh*-phrase and its trace. In minimalist terms, the application of Move raising α to the specifier of the matrix C in mapping (17a) to (17b), being an illegitimate step (violating the MLC), forms no chain. Since there is no morphological need to trigger further movement of any feature of α, all subsequent applications of Move leave α and t(α) unaffected. Therefore, the derivation of (16) yields an LF representation in which the quantifier α is not a member of any two-membered chain. Given that such an LF representation of (16) violates FI (vacuous quantification), the derivation of (16) crashes. This nonconvergent derivation of (16) exhibits severe deviance. That is, the derivation of (16), employing the application of Move raising the adjunct α to the specifier of the matrix C, which violates the MLC, necessarily yields an illegitimate LF representation (containing an illegitimate LF object, namely, the single-membered quantifier chain CH (how)); hence, the derivation of (16) crashes and exhibits severe deviance.

The chain formation analysis (incorporating the CFC) also captures the marginal deviance of (1b), repeated in (19).

(19) ??What$_1$ do you wonder [$_{CP}$ whether John fixed t$_1$]?

Recall that the derivation of (19) involves one illegitimate application of Move (violating the MLC). Consider the following mapping:

(20) a. [$_{CP}$ do [$_{TP}$ you wonder + v
[$_{CP}$ whether [$_{TP}$ John fixed + v [$_\alpha$ what]]]]]
b. [$_{CP}$ [$_\alpha$ what] [$_{C'}$ do [$_{TP}$ you wonder + v
[$_{CP}$ whether [$_{TP}$ John fixed + v t(α)]]]]]

In mapping (20a) to (20b), C$_{HL}$ employs an application of Move raising α to the specifier of the matrix C, which violates the MLC. Given the CFC, this illegitimate application of Move forms no chain. Later, in the LF component, however, C$_{HL}$ performs the following mapping (satisfying the MLC):

(21) a. [$_{CP}$[$_\alpha$ what] [$_{C'}$ do [$_{TP}$ you wonder + v
[$_{CP}$ whether [$_{TP}$ John fixed + v t(α)]]]]]
b. [$_{CP}$[$_\alpha$ what] [$_{C'}$ do [$_{TP}$ you wonder + v
[$_{CP}$ whether [$_{TP}$ John FF[α] + [fixed + v] t(α)]]]]]

In mapping (21a) to (21b), C$_{HL}$ employs an application of Move adjoining FF[α] to the complex head *fixed* + v to check the Case features of α and *fixed*. Recall that Case features are [−interpretable]; hence, they must be checked and erased before LF. Now notice that, given the chain formation algorithm, this single legitimate application of Move raising FF[α] can form not only the argument chain CH (FF[α], t(α)) but also the operator-variable chain CH (α, FF[α]) across the *wh*-island. That is, the derivation of (19), unlike the derivation of (16), yields an LF representation in which the quantifier α is a member of the two-membered chain CH (α, FF[α]). Given that such an LF representation of (19) satisfies FI, the derivation of (19) converges. This convergent derivation of (19) exhibits marginal deviance because of the single violation of the MLC. That is, the derivation of (19), employing the application of Move raising the object α to the specifier of the matrix C, which violates the MLC, still yields a legitimate LF representation. This convergent derivation of (19) exhibits marginal deviance as a result of employing one illegitimate step.

To highlight the central aspect of the chain formation analysis, let me illustrate schematically how C$_{HL}$ forms a chain headed by α, crossing an island for α.

Suppose C_{HL} constructs the following structure in which γ is an island for α:

(22) ... $[_\gamma$ ... β ... $[$ ... α ... $]$ ... $]$ ...

Given (22), the MLC analysis of island effects predicts that Move raising α out of γ (crossing $H(\gamma)$) violates the MLC. Now, suppose C_{HL} employs such an illegitimate application of Move raising α out of γ (crossing $H(\gamma)$). Then, C_{HL} yields (23).

(23) α ... $[_\gamma$ ... β ... $[$ ... $t(\alpha)$ ... $]$ ... $]$ ...

Given the CFC, this illegitimate application of Move raising α forms no chain. If all subsequent legitimate applications of Move leave α and $t(\alpha)$ unaffected, then C_{HL} yields an LF representation in which α is not a member of any two-membered chain. But if some subsequent legitimate application of Move affects $t(\alpha)$ and adjoins FF[α] to some higher category—say, β within γ (thereby satisfying the MLC)—then α will be a member of a two-membered chain formed by this legitimate application of Move. Suppose C_{HL} employs this legitimate application of Move adjoining FF[α] to β within γ. Then, C_{HL} yields (24).

(24) α ... $[_\gamma$ ... FF[α]$+\beta$ ... $[$ ... $t(\alpha)$ ... $]$ ... $]$ ...

Given the chain formation algorithm, this single legitimate application of Move raising FF[α] can form any number of chains each consisting of FF[α] and any other position associated with (a feature of) α, thereby forming two chains, CH (α, FF[α]) and CH (FF[α], $t(\alpha)$).

Under the chain formation analysis, therefore, the presence of $H(\gamma)$ constituting the intervening island γ for α does not necessarily prevent Move from forming a chain CH consisting of the two positions associated with some feature of α, separated by γ (i.e., CH (α, FF[α]) in (24)).

4.3.2 Subject versus Object

Let us extend the chain formation analysis to the severe deviance of (3a), repeated in (25).

(25) *What$_1$ do you wonder [$_{CP}$ whether t'_1 was fixed t_1]?

Recall that the derivation of (25) involves one illegitimate application of Move (violating the MLC). First consider the following mapping:

(26) a. [$_{TP}$ was fixed [$_\alpha$ what]]
      b. [$_{TP}$[$_\alpha$ what] [$_{T'}$ was fixed $t(\alpha)$]]

In mapping (26a) to (26b), C_{HL} employs an application of Move raising α to the specifier of T, which satisfies the MLC. This legitimate application of Move raising α forms the argument chain CH (α, t(α)). Later (but still) in the overt syntax, C_{HL} performs the following mapping:

(27) a. [$_{CP}$ do [$_{TP}$ you wonder + v

 [$_{CP}$ whether [$_{TP}$[$_α$ what] [$_{T'}$ was fixed t(α)]]]]]]

 b. [$_{CP}$[$_α$ what] [$_{C'}$ do [$_{TP}$ you wonder + v

 [$_{CP}$ whether [$_{TP}$ t'(α) [$_{T'}$ was fixed t(α)]]]]]]]

In mapping (27a) to (27b), C_{HL} employs an application of Move raising α from the embedded subject position to the specifier of the matrix C, which violates the MLC. Given the CFC, this illegitimate application of Move forms no chain. Since there is no morphological need to trigger further movement of any feature of α, all subsequent applications of Move leave α, t'(α), and t(α) unaffected. Note that the Case features of α and the embedded T were checked and erased when α was raised to the specifier of the embedded T. Therefore, the derivation of (25) yields an LF representation in which the quantifier α is not a member of any two-membered chain. Given that such an LF representation of (25) violates FI (vacuous quantification), the derivation of (25) crashes. This nonconvergent derivation of (25) exhibits severe deviance. That is, the derivation of (25), employing the application of Move raising α from the embedded subject position to the specifier of the matrix C, which violates the MLC, necessarily yields an illegitimate LF representation (containing an illegitimate LF object, namely, the single-membered quantifier chain CH (what)); hence, the derivation of (25) crashes and exhibits severe deviance.

Notice that the chain formation analysis of the severely deviant (25) crucially rests on the cyclic order of the two overt applications of Move raising *what*: passive movement precedes *wh*-movement. If the noncyclic order is permitted, the chain formation analysis makes a wrong prediction: (25) exhibits marginal deviance as a result of employing one illegitimate application of Move (violating the MLC). Consider the noncyclic derivation of (25) involving the following mapping:

(28) a. [$_{TP}$ was fixed [$_α$ what]]

 b. [$_{CP}$ C$_{wh}$ [$_{TP}$ was fixed [$_α$ what]]]

In mapping (28a) to (28b), C_{HL} concatenates C$_{wh}$ (bearing a strong *wh*-feature) and TP (whose head T bears a strong D-feature). At a later stage in this derivation, C_{HL} performs the following mapping:

(29) a. [$_{CP}$ do [$_{TP}$ you wonder + v
        [$_{CP}$ whether [$_{C'}$ C$_{wh}$ [$_{TP}$ was fixed [$_{α}$ what]]]]]]

   b. [$_{CP}$[$_{α}$ what] [$_{C'}$ do [$_{TP}$ you wonder + v
        [$_{CP}$ whether [$_{C'}$ C$_{wh}$ [$_{TP}$ was fixed t(α)]]]]]]

In mapping (29a) to (29b), C$_{HL}$ employs an application of Move raising α
from the embedded object position to the specifier of the matrix C, which
violates the MLC. Given the CFC, this illegitimate application of Move
forms no chain. However, this derivation, unlike its cyclic counterpart
discussed above, performs the following mapping (satisfying the MLC):

(30) a. [$_{CP}$[$_{α}$ what] [$_{C'}$ do [$_{TP}$ you wonder + v
        [$_{CP}$ whether [$_{C'}$ C$_{wh}$ [$_{TP}$ was fixed t(α)]]]]]]

   b. [$_{CP}$[$_{α}$ what] [$_{C'}$ do [$_{TP}$ you wonder + v
        [$_{CP}$ whether [$_{C'}$ C$_{wh}$ [$_{TP}$ t(α) [$_{T'}$ was fixed t'(α)]]]]]]]

In mapping (30a) to (30b), C$_{HL}$ employs an application of Move raising
t(α) to the specifier of the embedded T to check the Case features of α and
the embedded T. Recall that the D-feature of the embedded T is strong;
hence, it must be checked and erased before Spell-Out applies. Now
notice that, given the chain formation algorithm, this single legitimate
application of Move raising t(α) can form not only the argument chain
CH (t(α), t'(α)) but also the operator-variable chain CH (α, t(α)). That is,
the noncyclic derivation of (25), unlike its cyclic counterpart, yields an LF
representation in which the quantifier α is a member of the two-membered
chain CH (α, t(α)). Given that such an LF representation of (25) satisfies
FI, the noncyclic derivation of (25) converges. This convergent noncyclic
derivation of (25), if permitted, would exhibit marginal deviance because
of the single violation of the MLC, contrary to fact. Therefore, we must
exclude this convergent noncyclic derivation of (25).

   Note that neither the Shortest Derivation Condition (SDC) nor the
Strong Feature Condition (SFC) excludes the noncyclic derivation of
(25). The SDC requires that a derivation D perform cyclic applications
of Move only if D converges. Thus, the SDC cannot ensure the cyclic
order of the two overt applications of Move raising *what*, which forces the
derivation of (25) to crash. The SFC is divorced from the "strict cyclicity"
property of overt movement (see subsection 2.2.4). Thus, the SFC does
not ensure the cyclic order of the two overt applications of Move raising
what in the overt syntax.[8]

   To exclude the noncyclic derivation of (25), I appeal to the following
condition on concatenation:[9]

(31) α and β cannot be concatenated if some sublabel of α and some sublabel of β are both strong.

Given (31), C_{HL} cannot concatenate C_{wh} (bearing a strong *wh*-feature) and TP (whose head T bears a strong D-feature) in mapping (28a) to (28b): the convergent noncyclic derivation of (25) cannot be generated in the first place. Therefore, C_{HL} necessarily employs cyclic applications of Move raising *what* in the overt syntax: the nonconvergent cyclic derivation of (25) is forced by (31).

(31) is further supported by the following contrast (Chomsky and Lasnik 1993; Lasnik and Saito 1984, 1992):[10]

(32) a. *Who$_1$ do you wonder
         [$_{CP}$ whether [$_{TP}$ t$_1$ solved the problem]]?
     b. ??Who$_1$ do you wonder
         [$_{CP}$ whether John said [$_{CP}$[$_{TP}$ t$_1$ solved the problem]]]?

(32) shows that an MLC violation involving the subject of the clause headed by C_{wh} bearing a strong *wh*-feature is far more severe than an MLC violation involving the subject of the clause headed by C bearing no strong feature.

Given (31), first consider the relevant aspects of the derivation of the severely deviant (32a). At some point in the derivation, C_{HL} constructs the following structure:

(33) [$_{TP}$[$_{vP}$[$_\alpha$ who] solved + v the problem]]

Given the initial numeration of the derivation of (32a), the next step is either to raise α from the specifier of v to the specifier of T or to concatenate C_{wh} (bearing a strong *wh*-feature) and TP (whose head T bears a strong D-feature). Given (31), the second option is eliminated; hence, C_{HL} performs the first option, yielding (34).

(34) [$_{TP}$[$_\alpha$ who] [$_{T'}$[$_{vP}$ t(α) solved + v the problem]]]

At a later stage in this derivation, C_{HL} performs the following mapping:

(35) a. [$_{CP}$ do you wonder [$_{CP}$ whether
         [$_{TP}$[$_\alpha$ who] [$_{T'}$[$_{vP}$ t(α) solved + v the problem]]]]]
     b. [$_{CP}$[$_\alpha$ who] [$_{C'}$ do you wonder [$_{CP}$ whether
         [$_{TP}$ t'(α) [$_{T'}$[$_{vP}$ t(α) solved + v the problem]]]]]]

In mapping (35a) to (35b), C_{HL} employs an application of Move raising α from the embedded subject position to the specifier of the matrix C, which violates the MLC. Given the CFC, this illegitimate application of Move forms no chain. Since there is no morphological need to trigger further movement of any feature of α, all subsequent applications of Move leave α, $t'(\alpha)$, and $t(\alpha)$ unaffected. Note that the Case features of α and the embedded T were each checked and erased when α was raised to the specifier of the embedded T. Therefore, the derivation of (32a) yields an LF representation in which the quantifier α is not a member of any two-membered chain. Given that such an LF representation of (32a) violates FI (vacuous quantification), the derivation of (32a) crashes. This non-convergent derivation of (32a), forced to be cyclic by (31), exhibits severe deviance.

Now consider the relevant aspects of the derivation of the marginally deviant (32b). At some point in the derivation, C_{HL} constructs the following structure:

(36) $[_{TP}[_{vP}[_{\alpha}$ who] solved $+ v$ the problem]]

Given the initial numeration of the derivation of (32b), the next step is either to raise α from the specifier of v to the specifier of T or to concatenate C (bearing no strong feature) and TP (whose head T bears a strong D-feature). Notice that neither option violates (31). Suppose C_{HL} performs the second option. Then, C_{HL} yields (37).

(37) $[_{CP}$ C $[_{TP}[_{vP}[_{\alpha}$ who] solved $+ v$ the problem]]]

At a later stage in this derivation, C_{HL} performs the following mapping:

(38) a. $[_{CP}$ do you wonder $[_{CP}$ whether $[_{TP}$ John said
  $[_{CP}$ C $[_{TP}[_{vP}[_{\alpha}$ who] solved $+ v$ the problem]]]]]]]

   b. $[_{CP}[_{\alpha}$ who] $[_{C'}$ do you wonder $[_{CP}$ whether $[_{TP}$ John said
  $[_{CP}$ C $[_{TP}[_{vP}$ t(α) solved $+ v$ the problem]]]]]]]]

In mapping (38a) to (38b), C_{HL} employs an application of Move raising α from the specifier of the most deeply embedded v to the specifier of the matrix C, which violates the MLC. Given the CFC, this illegitimate application of Move forms no chain. However, this derivation, unlike the cyclic derivation of (32a), performs the following mapping (satisfying the MLC):

(39) a. $[_{CP}[_{\alpha}$ who] $[_{C'}$ do you wonder $[_{CP}$ whether $[_{TP}$ John said
  $[_{CP}$ C $[_{TP}[_{vP}$ t(α) solved $+ v$ the problem]]]]]]]

   b. $[_{CP}[_{\alpha}$ who] $[_{C'}$ do you wonder $[_{CP}$ whether $[_{TP}$ John said
  $[_{CP}$ C $[_{TP}$ t(α) $[_{T'}[_{vP}$ t$'(\alpha)$ solved $+ v$ the problem]]]]]]]]

In mapping (39a) to (39b), C_{HL} employs an application of Move raising $t(\alpha)$ to the specifier of the most deeply embedded T to check the Case features of α and the most deeply embedded T. Recall that the D-feature of the embedded T is strong; hence, it must be checked and erased before Spell-Out applies. Now notice that, given the chain formation algorithm, this single legitimate application of Move raising $t(\alpha)$ can form not only the argument chain CH $(t(\alpha), t'(\alpha))$ but also the operator-variable chain CH $(\alpha, t(\alpha))$. That is, the noncyclic derivation of (32b), unlike the cyclic derivation of (32a), yields an LF representation in which the quantifier α is a member of the two-membered chain CH $(\alpha, t(\alpha))$. Given that such an LF representation of (32b) satisfies FI, the noncyclic derivation of (32b) converges. This convergent derivation of (32b), permitted to be noncyclic by (31), exhibits marginal deviance because of the single violation of the MLC.[11]

As shown above, the condition on concatenation (formulated as (31)) forces the derivation of (32a) to be cyclic, while permitting the derivation of (32b) to be noncyclic. The cyclic derivation of (32a), employing the application of Move raising α from the specifier of the embedded T to the specifier of the matrix C, which violates the MLC, necessarily yields an illegitimate LF representation (containing an illegitimate LF object, namely, the single-membered operator chain CH (who)); hence, the derivation of (32a) (satisfying (31)) crashes and exhibits severe deviance. By contrast, the noncyclic derivation of (32b), employing the application of Move raising α from the specifier of the most deeply embedded v to the specifier of the matrix C, which violates the MLC, still yields a legitimate LF representation. This convergent derivation of (32b) (satisfying (31)) exhibits marginal deviance as a result of employing one illegitimate step. Under the chain formation analysis, therefore, the contrast in (32) receives a principled account.

The chain formation analysis also captures the severe deviance exhibited by superraising cases such as (40) (Lasnik and Saito 1992).

(40) *John$_1$ seems that it was told t_1 that Mary was intelligent.

The derivation of the severely deviant (40) involves one illegitimate application of Move (violating the MLC). Consider the following mapping:

(41) a. $[_{TP}$ seems $+ v$ $[_{CP}$ that $[_{TP}$ it was told $[_\alpha$ John$]$
$[_{CP}$ that $[_{TP}$ Mary was intelligent$]]]]]$

b. $[_{TP}[_\alpha$ John$]$ $[_{T'}$ seems $+$ v $[_{CP}$ that $[_{TP}$ it was told t(α)
$[_{CP}$ that $[_{TP}$ Mary was intelligent$]]]]]]$

In mapping (41a) to (41b), C_{HL} employs an application of Move raising α to the specifier of the matrix T, which violates the MLC. Given the CFC, this illegitimate application of Move forms no chain. Since there is no morphological need to trigger further movement of any feature of α, all subsequent applications of Move leave α and t(α) unaffected. Therefore, the derivation of (40) yields an LF representation in which the argument α does not terminate in a θ-marked position.[12] Given that such an LF representation of (40) violates FI (a θ-Criterion violation), the derivation of (40) crashes. This nonconvergent derivation of (40) exhibits severe deviance. That is, the derivation of (40), employing the application of Move raising α from the embedded object position to the matrix subject position (superraising), which violates the MLC, necessarily yields an illegitimate LF representation (containing an illegitimate LF object, namely, the non-θ-marked argument chain CH (John)); hence, the derivation of (40) crashes and exhibits severe deviance.

4.3.3   Object versus Quasi Object

As we have seen so far, the derivations of (16), (25), (32a), and (40), which employ an illegitimate application of Move raising α followed by no legitimate application of Move affecting t(α), yield an illegitimate LF representation and crash, whereas the derivations of (19) and (32b), which employ an illegitimate application of Move raising α followed by a legitimate application of Move affecting t(α), yield a legitimate LF representation and converge. This analysis is further supported by the contrast in (5), repeated in (42).

(42) a.   *How many pounds$_1$ do you wonder
            $[_{CP}$ whether John weighed t$_1]$?

    b.   ??What$_1$ do you wonder
            $[_{CP}$ whether John weighed t$_1]$?

(42) shows that the MLC violation involving the quasi object *how many pounds* is far more severe than the MLC violation involving the object *what*. To provide a principled account of this contrast, I appeal to the following independently motivated Case-theoretic distinction: objects have Case features, whereas quasi objects do not. This Case-theoretic distinction is motivated by the following contrast:

(43) a. *150 pounds was/were weighed by John.
    b. The potatoes were weighed by John.

First consider the derivation of the severely deviant (43a). Given that the quasi object *150 pounds* has no Case feature, the raising of the quasi object bearing no Case feature to the specifier of T fails to check the Case feature of T: the Case feature of T ([−interpretable]) survives intact to LF. Given that such an LF representation of (43a) violates FI, the derivation of (43a) crashes. This nonconvergent derivation of (43a) exhibits severe deviance. By contrast, the derivation of (43b) converges. Given that the object *the potatoes* has a Case feature, the raising of the object bearing the Case feature to the specifier of T checks the Case feature of T: the Case features of the object and T are checked and erased before LF. Given that such an LF representation of (43b) satisfies FI, the derivation of (43b) converges. This convergent derivation of (43b) exhibits no deviance.[13,14]

Given this Case-theoretic distinction between objects and quasi objects, let us return to the derivation of the severely deviant (42a). Consider the following mapping:

(44) a. $[_{CP}$ do $[_{TP}$ you wonder $+ v$
      $[_{CP}$ whether $[_{TP}$ John weighed $+ v$ $[_\alpha$ how many pounds]]]]]]
    b. $[_{CP}[_\alpha$ how many pounds] $[_{C'}$ do $[_{TP}$ you wonder $+ v$
      $[_{CP}$ whether $[_{TP}$ John weighed $+ v$ $t(\alpha)$]]]]]]

In mapping (44a) to (44b), C_{HL} employs an application of Move raising α to the specifier of the matrix C, which violates the MLC. Given the CFC, this illegitimate application of Move forms no chain. Since there is no morphological need to trigger further movement of any feature of α, all subsequent applications of Move leave α and $t(\alpha)$ unaffected. Note that the quasi object α has no Case feature. Therefore, the derivation of (42a) yields an LF representation in which the quantifier α is not a member of any two-membered chain. Given that such an LF representation of (42a) violates FI (vacuous quantification), the derivation of (42a) crashes. This nonconvergent derivation of (42a) exhibits severe deviance.

Turning to the derivation of the marginally deviant (42b), first consider the following mapping:

(45) a. $[_{CP}$ do $[_{TP}$ you wonder $+ v$
      $[_{CP}$ whether $[_{TP}$ John weighed $+ v$ $[_\alpha$ what]]]]]]
    b. $[_{CP}[_\alpha$ what] $[_{C'}$ do $[_{TP}$ you wonder $+ v$
      $[_{CP}$ whether $[_{TP}$ John weighed $+ v$ $t(\alpha)$]]]]]]

In mapping (45a) to (45b), C_{HL} employs an application of Move raising α to the specifier of the matrix C, which violates the MLC. Given the CFC, this illegitimate application of Move forms no chain. Later, in the LF component, however, C_{HL} performs the following mapping (satisfying the MLC):

(46) a. $[_{CP}[_\alpha$ what$]$ $[_{C'}$ do $[_{TP}$ you wonder $+ v$
          $[_{CP}$ whether $[_{TP}$ John [weighed $+ v$] t(α)]]]]]
     b. $[_{CP}[_\alpha$ what$]$ $[_{C'}$ do $[_{TP}$ you wonder $+ v$
          $[_{CP}$ whether $[_{TP}$ John FF[α] $+$ [weighed $+ v$] t(α)]]]]]

In mapping (46a) to (46b), C_{HL} employs an application of Move adjoining FF[α] to the complex head *weighed* $+ v$ to check the Case features of α and *weighed*. Recall that, unlike the quasi object *how many pounds*, the object *what* has a Case feature that must be checked and erased before LF. Now notice that, given the chain formation algorithm, this single legitimate application of Move raising FF[α] can form not only the argument chain CH (FF[α], t(α)) but also the operator-variable chain CH (α, FF[α]). That is, the derivation of (42b), unlike the derivation of (42a), yields an LF representation in which the quantifier α is a member of the two-membered chain CH (α, FF[α]). Given that such an LF representation of (42b) satisfies FI, the derivation of (42b) converges. This convergent derivation of (42b) exhibits marginal deviance because of the single violation of the MLC.

To summarize, the chain formation analysis captures the contrast between the severely deviant (42a) and the marginally deviant (42b) as follows. The derivation of (42a), employing the application of Move raising the quasi object α to the specifier of the matrix C, which violates the MLC, necessarily yields an illegitimate LF representation (containing an illegitimate LF object, namely, the single-membered operator chain CH (how many pounds)); hence, the derivation of (42a) crashes and exhibits severe deviance. By contrast, the derivation of (42b), employing the application of Move raising the object α to the specifier of the matrix C, which violates the MLC, still yields a legitimate LF representation. This convergent derivation of (42b) exhibits marginal deviance as a result of employing one illegitimate step.

In this section, I developed the chain formation analysis, which captures degrees of deviance exhibited by derivations employing only one illegitimate application of Move (violating the MLC): the increased deviance of (16), (25), (32a), (40), and (42a), in contrast to the marginal deviance of (19), (32b) and (42b), results from the failure of convergence (in addition to the single violation of the MLC).

4.4 Further Consequences

The chain formation analysis of degrees of deviance is further supported by the contrast between (47) and (48).

(47) a. *Why$_1$ do you wonder [$_{CP}$ whether John fixed the car t$_1$]?
    b. *How$_1$ do you wonder [$_{CP}$ whether John fixed the car t$_1$]?

(48) a. ??Where$_1$ do you wonder [$_{CP}$ whether John fixed the car t$_1$]?
    b. ??When$_1$ do you wonder [$_{CP}$ whether John fixed the car t$_1$]?

As these examples show, an MLC violation involving *wh*-phrases such as *why* and *how* is far more severe than an MLC violation involving *wh*-phrases such as *where* and *when*.

To capture this contrast, let us first recall Huang's (1982) null preposition analysis. He provides the following two facts: (a) *where* and *when*, unlike *why* and *how*, can appear as a complement of a preposition (e.g., *from where* and *since when*), and (b) *there* and *then* can be analyzed as pronominal forms of *where* and *when*, whereas no corresponding pronominal form exists for *how* and *why*. On the basis of these facts, he proposes that *where* and *when* are categories that can appear as a complement of a phonetically null preposition *p*, as in (49).[15]

(49) a. [$_{PP}$ *p* where]
    b. [$_{PP}$ *p* when]

Given that the null preposition *p*, just like other prepositions, has a Case feature, its complement (e.g., *where*, *when*) also has a Case feature. Such Case features, being [−interpretable], must be checked and erased before LF.

Given the null preposition analysis, let us return to the derivation of the severely deviant (47a). Consider the following mapping:

(50) a. [$_{CP}$ do [$_{TP}$ you wonder + *v*
        [$_{CP}$ whether [$_{TP}$ John fixed + *v* the car [$_{α}$ why]]]]]
    b. [$_{CP}$[$_{α}$ why] [$_{C'}$ do [$_{TP}$ you wonder + *v*
        [$_{CP}$ whether [$_{TP}$ John fixed + *v* the car t($α$)]]]]]

In mapping (50a) to (50b), C$_{HL}$ employs an application of Move raising $α$ to the specifier of the matrix C, which violates the MLC. Given the CFC, this illegitimate application of Move forms no chain. Since there is no morphological need to trigger further movement of any feature of α, all subsequent applications of Move leave α and t(α) unaffected. Note that the adjunct *why* has no Case feature. Therefore, the derivation of (47a) yields an LF representation in which the quantifier α is not a member of any two-membered chain. Given that such an LF representation of (47a) violates FI (vacuous quantification), the derivation of (47a) crashes. This nonconvergent derivation of (47a) exhibits severe deviance. That is, the derivation of (47a), employing the application of Move raising the adjunct α to the specifier of the matrix C, which violates the MLC, necessarily yields an illegitimate LF representation (containing an illegitimate LF object, namely, the single-membered operator chain CH (why)); hence, the derivation of (47a) crashes and exhibits severe deviance. The same analysis holds for the derivation of the severely deviant (47b) (see the discussion below (16)).

Turning to the derivation of the marginally deviant (48a), first consider the following mapping:

(51) a. [$_{CP}$ do [$_{TP}$ you wonder + v
        [$_{CP}$ whether [$_{TP}$ John fixed + v the car [$_{PP}$ p [$_{\alpha}$ where]]]]]]

    b. [$_{CP}$[$_{\alpha}$ where] [$_{C'}$ do [$_{TP}$ you wonder + v
        [$_{CP}$ whether [$_{TP}$ John fixed + v the car [$_{PP}$ p t(α)]]]]]]

In mapping (51a) to (51b), C_{HL} employs an application of Move raising α to the specifier of the matrix C, which violates the MLC. Given the CFC, this illegitimate application of Move forms no chain. Later, in the LF component, however, C_{HL} performs the following mapping (satisfying the MLC):

(52) a. [$_{CP}$[$_{\alpha}$ where] [$_{C'}$ do [$_{TP}$ you wonder + v
        [$_{CP}$ whether [$_{TP}$ John fixed + v the car [$_{PP}$ p t(α)]]]]]]

    b. [$_{CP}$[$_{\alpha}$ where] [$_{C'}$ do [$_{TP}$ you wonder + v
        [$_{CP}$ whether [$_{TP}$ John fixed + v the car [$_{PP}$ FF[α] + p t(α)]]]]]]

In mapping (52a) to (52b), C_{HL} employs an application of Move adjoining FF[α] to the null preposition p to check the Case features of α and p. Recall that the prepositional complement *where* (appearing as the complement of the null preposition p) has a Case feature that must be checked and erased before LF. Now notice that, given the chain formation algorithm, this single legitimate application of Move raising FF[α] can form not only the argument chain CH (FF[α], t(α)) but also the operator-variable chain CH (α, FF[α]). That is, the derivation of (48a), unlike the derivations of (47a–b), yields an LF representation in which the quantifier α is a member of the two-membered chain CH (α, FF[α]). Given that such an LF representation of (48a) satisfies FI, the derivation of (48a) converges. This convergent derivation of (48a) exhibits marginal deviance because of the single violation of the MLC. That is, the derivation of (48a), employing the application of Move raising the prepositional complement α to the specifier of the matrix C, which violates the MLC, still yields a legitimate LF representation. This convergent derivation of (48a) exhibits marginal deviance as a result of employing one illegitimate step. The same analysis holds for the derivation of the marginally deviant (48b).

The chain formation analysis similarly captures the marginal deviance exhibited by cases such as (53).

(53) ??Whom$_1$ do you wonder [$_{CP}$ whether John spoke to t$_1$]?

The derivation of (53), like the derivations of (48a–b), employs one illegitimate application of Move (involving prepositional complements) and exhibits marginal deviance. First consider the following mapping:

(54) a. [$_{CP}$ do [$_{TP}$ you wonder $+ v$
    [$_{CP}$ whether [$_{TP}$ John spoke $+ v$ [$_{PP}$ to [$_\alpha$ whom]]]]]]]
  b. [$_{CP}$[$_\alpha$ whom] [$_{C'}$ do [$_{TP}$ you wonder $+ v$
    [$_{CP}$ whether [$_{TP}$ John spoke $+ v$ [$_{PP}$ to t(α)]]]]]]]

In mapping (54a) to (54b), C$_{HL}$ employs an application of Move raising α to the specifier of the matrix C, which violates the MLC. Given the CFC, this illegitimate application of Move forms no chain. Later, in the LF component, however, C$_{HL}$ performs the following mapping (satisfying the MLC):

(55) a. [$_{CP}$[$_\alpha$ whom] [$_{C'}$ do [$_{TP}$ you wonder $+ v$
    [$_{CP}$ whether [$_{TP}$ John spoke $+ v$ [$_{PP}$ to t(α)]]]]]]]
  b. [$_{CP}$[$_\alpha$ whom] [$_{C'}$ do [$_{TP}$ you wonder $+ v$
    [$_{CP}$ whether [$_{TP}$ John spoke $+ v$ [$_{PP}$ FF[α] $+$ to t(α)]]]]]]]

In mapping (55a) to (55b), C$_{HL}$ employs an application of Move adjoining FF[α] to the preposition *to* to check the Case features of α and *to*. Recall that the prepositional complement *whom* (appearing as the complement of the preposition *to*) has a Case feature that must be checked and erased before LF. Now notice that, given the chain formation algorithm, this single legitimate application of Move raising FF[α] can form not only the argument chain CH (FF[α], t(α)) but also the operator-variable chain CH (α, FF[α]). That is, the derivation of (53), like the derivations of (48a–b), yields an LF representation in which the quantifier α is a member of the two-membered chain CH (α, FF[α]). Given that such an LF representation of (53) satisfies FI, the derivation of (53) converges. This convergent derivation of (53) exhibits marginal deviance because of the single violation of the MLC. That is, the derivation of (53), employing the application of Move raising the prepositional complement α to the specifier of the matrix C, which violates the MLC, still yields a legitimate LF representation. This convergent derivation of (53) exhibits marginal deviance as a result of employing one illegitimate step.

Finally, let us examine the following derivation, which employs one illegitimate application of Move (involving a verbal complement) and induces a greater degree of deviance than does the derivation of the marginally deviant (53):[16]

(56) *?To whom$_1$ do you wonder [$_{CP}$ whether John spoke t$_1$]?

To provide a principled account for the increased deviance of (56), we need a better understanding of the property of *optional pied-piping* exhibited by the derivations of (53) and (56): the prepositional complement *whom* undergoes *wh*-movement in the derivation of (53), whereas the verbal complement *to whom* undergoes *wh*-movement in the derivation of (56). Let us first examine the following case of optional pied-piping exhibited by nondeviant pairs such as (57a–b):

(57) a. I wonder [$_{CP}$[$_{DP}$ whom]$_1$ John spoke [$_{PP}$ to t$_1$]].
      b. I wonder [$_{CP}$[$_{PP}$ to whom]$_1$ John spoke t$_1$].

In the derivations of (57a–b), the embedded C has a strong feature triggering *wh*-movement; hence, the embedded C raises the *wh*-feature of *whom*. Recall that in the overt syntax, Move raises the smallest category containing the *wh*-feature of *whom* for the derivations of (57a–b) to converge (Chomsky 1995, 262), and I have suggested that the SDC in effect requires such minimization.[17] Given this, we must say that the prepositional complement *whom* is the smallest category containing the *wh*-feature of *whom* for the derivation of (57a) to converge, whereas the verbal complement *to whom* is the smallest category containing the *wh*-feature of *whom* for the derivation of (57b) to converge.[18] I assume the smallest category containing the *wh*-feature of *whom* to be a category bearing the *wh*-feature as its sublabel. To be concrete, I propose the following condition:

(58) If β is determined to be the smallest category containing FF[α] for convergence, FF[α] is understood to be a sublabel of β.

Given (58), in the derivation of (57a), FF[whom] is understood to be a sublabel of the prepositional complement *whom*, whereas in the derivation of (57b), FF[whom] is understood to be a sublabel of the verbal complement *to whom*.

Given the analysis of optional pied-piping (incorporating (58)), let us examine the derivation of (56) (which induces a greater degree of deviance than does the derivation of the marginally deviant (53)). Consider the following mapping:

(59) a. [$_{CP}$ do [$_{TP}$ you wonder + v
[$_{CP}$ whether [$_{TP}$ John spoke + v [$_α$ to whom]]]]]
b. [$_{CP}$[$_α$ to whom] [$_{C'}$ do [$_{TP}$ you wonder + v
[$_{CP}$ whether [$_{TP}$ John spoke + v t(α)]]]]]

Suppose, in mapping (59a) to (59b), C_{HL} analyzes α as the smallest category containing FF[whom] for the derivation of (56) to converge. Then, the SDC in effect forces Move to raise α to the specifier of the matrix C, which violates the MLC. Given the CFC, this illegitimate application of Move forms no chain. Now notice that, given (58), FF[whom] is understood to be a sublabel of α, α a verbal complement the head of which is a preposition *to*. That is, FF[whom] is analyzed as being in the position adjoined to the preposition *to*. Recall that such an adjoined position is a member of the checking domain of *to*. Given this, the Case feature of *whom* in FF[whom] is analyzed as already being in the checking domain of *to* (and the Case features of *whom* and *to* are presumably erased); hence, C_{HL} need not employ an application of Move adjoining FF[whom] to the preposition *to* (to check the Case features of *to* and *whom*). If so, there is no morphological need to trigger further movement of any feature of α; hence, all subsequent applications of Move leave α and t(α) unaffected. Therefore, the derivation of (56) yields an LF representation in which the quantifier α is not a member of any two-membered chain. Given that such an LF representation of (56) violates FI (vacuous quantification), the derivation of (56), unlike the derivation of (53), crashes. This nonconvergent derivation of (56) exhibits severe deviance.

Two problems undermine this analysis of (56). First, the deviance of (56) is not as severe as the deviance induced by the nonconvergent derivations of (47a–b), which could mean that C_{HL} generates a convergent derivation of (56). Second, if the derivation of (56) (taking the verbal complement *to whom* to be the smallest category containing FF[whom]) crashes, then under the SDC analysis, C_{HL} can take some other category to be the smallest category containing FF[whom] and should seek a convergent derivation of (56).

To provide a unified account of these two problems, I propose that the observed deviance of (56) may be attributed to the presence of a convergent but less optimal derivation of (56) (violating the MLC). I demonstrate that such a derivation of (56) takes the prepositional complement *whom* to be the smallest category containing FF[whom] but raises the verbal complement *to whom*.

Suppose, in mapping (59a) to (59b), C_{HL} analyzes the prepositional complement *whom* as the smallest category containing FF[whom] for the derivation of (56) to converge. Then, the SDC, in effect, prohibits Move from raising the verbal complement α, which is larger than the smallest category containing FF[whom], namely, the prepositional complement *whom*. However, such an application of Move (inducing a violation of the SDC) does not prevent the derivation of (56) from yielding a legitimate LF representation. That is, the derivation of (56), employing this illegitimate step (violating the MLC and leading to the less economical path), must covertly adjoin FF[whom] (contained in t(α)) to the preposition *to* for the checking of Case features, thereby forming the operator-variable chain and circumventing a violation of FI at LF. Notice that the prepositional complement *whom* is taken to be the smallest category containing FF[whom]; hence, FF[whom] is understood to be a sublabel of the prepositional complement *whom*, not a sublabel of the verbal complement *to whom*. Given this, the Case feature of *whom* in FF[whom] is not analyzed as already being in the checking domain of the preposition *to*; hence, C_{HL} must covertly adjoin FF[whom] to the preposition *to* (to check the case features of *whom* and *to*). This convergent derivation of (56) (taking the prepositional complement *whom* to be the smallest category containing FF[whom] but raising the verbal complement *to whom*) exhibits deviance induced by the violations of the MLC and the SDC, which is naturally more severe than the deviance induced by the violation of the MLC (see the convergent derivation of (53) taking the prepositional complement *whom* to be the smallest category containing FF[whom] and raising *whom*), but (I speculate) less severe than the deviance induced by the violations of the MLC and FI (see the nonconvergent derivations of (47a–b)).[19]

In this section, I demonstrated that under the chain formation analysis (incorporating (58)), the severe deviance of (47a–b), in contrast to the marginal deviance of (48a–b), results from the failure of convergence (in addition to the single violation of the MLC). I attributed the slightly increased deviance of (56), in contrast to the marginal deviance of (53), to the presence of a convergent but less optimal derivation of (56).

4.5 Summary

In this chapter, I argued that the chain formation analysis captures the contrast between objects (including prepositional complements such as *whom* in (53)), on the one hand, and adjuncts, subjects, and quasi objects (including verbal complements such as *to whom* in (56)), on the other. I showed that all the severely deviant cases involve a violation of FI at LF (in addition to a violation of the MLC); consequently, their derivations crash, thereby inducing severe deviance. The chain formation analysis achieves significant generality and simplicity by appealing to already existing, independently motivated Case-theoretic distinctions (concerning noncyclic applicability of the operation Move).

Notes

Chapter 1

1. As this monograph was being completed, Brody 1995 appeared, which I am not able to examine here. For discussion of the topics related to his analysis, see Epstein et al. 1995.

2. See Chomsky 1993 for detailed discussion of the elimination of D-Structure and S-Structure as linguistic levels. See also Brody 1993 for relevant discussion.

3. In fact, economy conditions hold only among convergent derivations. Thus, if a derivation crashes, it does not block others (Chomsky 1995, 220).

4. The highly descriptive formulation of the SFC given in (2) will be simplified in subsection 2.2.4.

5. See Jackendoff 1977 and Stowell 1981 for the development of the X-bar-theoretic format. For preminimalist reduction of bar levels to relational properties, see, among others, Freidin 1992, Fukui and Speas 1986, Muysken 1982, Oishi 1990, and Speas 1986, 1990.

6. Merge substitutes a newly constructed syntactic object K for (α, β).

7. In section 2.1, the "strict cyclicity" property of merger will be discussed in light of derivational economy.

8. Move substitutes a newly constructed syntactic object Σ' for Σ.

9. Erase substitutes a newly constructed syntactic object Σ' for Σ.

10. In chapter 2, the syntactic operations Merge, Move, and Erase and their functions will be discussed in greater detail.

11. For a different proposal deriving the X-bar schemata, see Kayne 1993, 1994. See also Chomsky 1994, 1995 for relevant discussion of the central aspects of Kayne's proposal.

12. For relevant discussion of the articulated IP structure, see, among others, Belletti 1990, Chomsky 1991, 1993, Chomsky and Lasnik 1993, Iatridou 1990, and Pollock 1989.

13. For relevant discussion of "Larsonian shell" structure analyses, see, among others, Chomsky 1993, 1994, 1995, Hale and Keyser 1993, Larson 1988, 1990.

14. For relevant discussion of other predicate-internal subject analyses, see Collins and Thráinsson 1993, Fukui and Speas 1986, Kitagawa 1986, Koizumi 1993, 1995, Koopman and Sportiche 1991, Kuroda 1988.

15. For relevant discussion of constructions such as (22a–b), see Jonas 1995, 1996, Jonas and Bobaljik 1993.

16. Constructions such as (22a–b) and their derivations will be extensively discussed in chapter 2.

17. Chomsky (1995, 358) points out that the shifting of Obj can precede the concatenation of Subj and a projection of v if the $v - V^{max}$ configuration is allowed to assign the θ-role of the external argument of V to any specifier position of v (including the outer specifier of v). This analysis, dispensing with the notion "equidistance," no longer captures the correlation of verb movement and object shift (Holmberg's (1986) generalization). See Jonas 1995, 1996 for detailed discussion of equidistance phenomena and her arguments against the shifting of Obj to the (inner) specifier of v (prior to the concatenation of Subj and a projection of v).

18. Note that unlike Chomsky's (1993) analysis, his (1994, 1995) analysis incorporates the notion "include," to define relevant domains.

19. The "one-step" erasure process I am assuming here is given in (i).

(i) Checked α is erased when possible.

(i) is a simplified version of Chomsky's (1995, 280) "two-step" erasure process, given in (ii).

(ii) a. Checked α is deleted when possible.
    b. Deleted α is erased when possible.

Chomsky proposes that deletion makes α invisible at the interface but accessible to C_{HL}, whereas erasure eliminates α entirely, so that α is inaccessible to C_{HL}, not just to interpretability at the interface. To the best of my understanding, the difference between (i) and (ii) does not affect any of my proposals; hence, I adopt the simpler "one-step" erasure process given in (i).

20. Chomsky (1993, 32) states that "operations are driven by morphological necessity: certain features must be checked in the checking domain of a head, or the derivation will crash." Under the framework of Chomsky 1995, strong features and [−interpretable] features must be checked, and the necessity of checking them drives the syntactic operations Merge, Move, and Erase.

21. For a recent proposal concerning the deduction of empirically desirable aspects of (25), see Epstein 1994, 1995, and Epstein et al. 1995.

22. In chapter 2, I will discuss some desirable consequences of taking the head of the target (rather than the target itself) to be an attracting category.

23. The principle *Greed* (Chomsky 1993, 1994) is eliminated in favor of LR. For relevant discussion of the formulation of LR, see Chomsky 1995 and Lasnik 1995b.

24. In chapter 3, various movement phenomena are shown to receive a unified analysis in terms of the MLC.

25. Chomsky (1995, 356) later presents a revised version of (31), which, as he notes, loses the correlation between verb movement and object shift (Holmberg's (1986) generalization). In this study, I adopt (31).

26. The adverb *ekki* (base-generated inside the v^{max}) is ignored in the tree representations below.

27. Following Chomsky (1995), I assume that an argument α can enter into a checking relation only if α is a nontrivial chain. Given this, Subj, being a trivial chain, cannot enter into a checking relation when introduced into a tree (e.g., (33)).

28. The MLC does not prohibit T from attracting Obj in (35), but the concatenation of Obj and T^{max} necessarily renders the derivation less economical (see section 1.7).

29. In chapter 4, I will examine what counts as a legitimate LF object, and how such an LF object is generated.

30. Chomsky (1995, 220) states that C_{HL} generates the three relevant sets of derivations: the set D of derivations; a subset D_C of convergent derivations of D; and a subset D_A of admissible derivations of D. Economy of representation determines D_C, whereas economy of derivation determines D_A. Finally, D_A is a subset of D_C.

31. Chomsky (1993, 30) suggests that "[t]he intuitive idea is that LF operations are a kind of 'wired-in' reflex, operating mechanically beyond any directly observable effects. They are less costly than overt operations. The system tries to reach PF 'as fast as possible,' minimizing overt syntax."

32. In chapter 2, I argue that Procrastinate is eliminable: the empirically desirable aspects of Procrastinate (e.g., the timing of verb movement) are deducible on independent grounds (see section 2.3).

33. The restriction on derivation length was first proposed as a general guideline eliminating unnecessary steps in a given derivation (Chomsky 1991) and later elaborated as a more articulated economy principle that, interacting with other economy principle(s), determines an interpretation of derivational economy (see, among others, Chomsky 1993, 1994, 1995; Collins 1994; Epstein 1992; Kitahara 1994b, 1995).

Chapter 2

1. For discussion of the "binary" property of merger, see Collins 1995.

2. In mapping (8a) to (8b), C_{HL} performs the following two steps. The first step takes α and β and concatenates them, forming L, as in (i).

(i) $\alpha, \beta \longrightarrow$

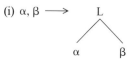

The second step takes L and Σ and replaces β in Σ by L, forming Σ′, as in (ii).

(ii) L,

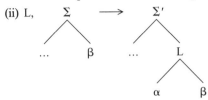

3. In mapping (13a) to (13b), C_{HL} performs the following two steps. The first step takes K (containing α) and concatenates K and α, forming L, as in (i).

(i)

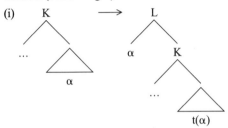

The second step takes L and Σ and replaces K in Σ by L, forming Σ′, as in (ii).

(ii)

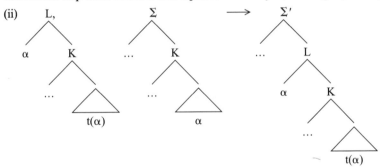

4. Assuming that a derivation involving noncyclic concatenation (e.g., noncyclic application of Move) fails to yield a single representation, I have argued (Kitahara 1994b) that the absence of noncyclic concatenation is deducible from the *Single Representation Requirement* (SRR) (which requires the root to reflexively dominate every category). Collins (1995), incorporating a similar assumption, deduces the absence of noncyclic concatenation from the principle *Integration* (which requires that every category (except the root) must be contained in another category). Chomsky's (1994, 1995) analysis, however, has no such problem (concerning noncyclic application of Move). That is, given his definition of Move (stated in (9)), a derivation involving noncyclic application of Move can still yield a single representation (thereby satisfying the SRR or Integration). See also Bobaljik 1995 and Watanabe 1995 for recent proposals on topics related to cyclic and noncyclic concatenation.

5. For discussion of topics related to derivation length, see also Kitahara 1994b, 1995.

6. For detailed discussion of island phenomena, see, among others, Chomsky 1973, 1981, Huang 1982, Ross 1967.

7. Following Freidin (1978), Browning (1991) argues that the principle of *strict cyclicity* can be eliminated in favor of the *Subjacency Condition* formulated as a constraint on S-Structure representation. One of the minimalist assumptions that I adopt here is that S-Structure (like D-Structure) is eliminated as a level of representation. Given this assumption, there cannot be any S-Structure conditions (including the Subjacency Condition formulated as such).

8. See Chomsky 1993 for detailed discussion of the elimination of both D-Structure and S-Structure.

9. Under Chomsky's (1993) proposal, applications of GT introducing adjuncts or applying in the LF component are, by pure stipulation, exempted from the EC. For further discussion of such undesirable aspects of the EC, see Kitahara 1994b, 1995.

10. Recall that under the framework of Chomsky 1994, 1995, Merge is defined so as to operate on two separate phrase markers and to apply at the root only (cyclic application).

11. The Subject Condition remains axiomatic under the Minimalist Program (Chomsky 1993, 1994, 1995). For related discussion of Subject Condition effects, see, among others, Chomsky 1973, Collins 1994, Huang 1982, Kawashima 1994, Lasnik and Saito 1984, 1992. See also Kitahara 1994b for an Agr-based analysis of such effects.

12. For recent discussion of the so-called Condition on Extraction Domain (CED) phenomena including the subject island violation (25) (Huang 1982), see Epstein et al. 1995, Takahashi 1994, Toyoshima 1996.

13. Under a slightly different set of assumptions, Collins (1994) proposes a theory of derivational economy under which the cyclic derivation of (25), which violates the Subject Condition, is forced. See also Kitahara 1995 for an economy-based analysis of (19) and (25) within the framework of Chomsky 1993.

14. One of the minimalist assumptions that I adopt here is that each instance of movement (triggered by the necessity of feature checking) is "one-step" movement directly to a position in which feature checking takes place; hence, all intermediate traces are absent in the structures. As far as I can see, this simplification does not affect any of the arguments presented here. For further discussion concerning successive-cyclic movement, see, among others, Abe 1993, 1996, Chomsky 1991, 1993, 1994, 1995, Collins 1994, 1995, Torrego 1984, Takahashi 1994.

15. Kawashima and Kitahara (1996) and Groat (1995b) independently point out that the empirically desirable aspects of strict cyclicity are also deducible from the *Linear Correspondence Axiom* (Kayne 1993, 1994), interpreted in terms of the derivational definition of c-command (Epstein 1994, 1995). For further discussion of strict cyclicity within the "derivational c-command" analysis, see Epstein et al. 1995.

16. This means that for any LI (with both phonetic and semantic features), (a) LI is pronounced only once at PF, and (b) LI is interpreted only once at LF.

17. The elimination of PF[α] from either α or t(α) is arguably forced by linear ordering considerations. The leading idea of the linear ordering analysis proposed by Kayne (1993, 1994) and subsequently elaborated by Chomsky (1994, 1995) is stated in (i).

(i) The syntactic relation "asymmetrical c-command" imposes a linear ordering of terminal elements (bearing phonetic features); any phrase marker that violates it is barred.

Assuming that α and t(α) are two instances of a single category, the linear ordering analysis requires that neither α nor t(α) enters into an "asymmetrical c-command" relation with the other (meaning that a category cannot precede or follow itself when linearly ordered); consequently, PF[α] must be eliminated from either α or t(α) (along with many other features). See Nuñes 1995 for further discussion of this point.

18. Following Chomsky (1995), I limit the ensuing discussion to a syntactic procedure, namely, a computation from N to λ.

19. Note that the head of CH (LI, t(LI)) receives some semantic interpretation in certain cases (e.g., definite nominals; Diesing 1992). Such semantic interpretation may be attributed to the [+interpretable] features of FF[LI] in the head of CH, which survive to LF.

20. See, among others, Emonds 1978, Pollock 1989, Chomsky 1991 for pre-minimalist analyses of verb movement.

21. The trace of the subject occupying the specifier of v is omitted when irrelevant.

22. Recall that under the "Larsonian shell" analysis of transitive verb constructions (Chomsky 1995), the main verb V overtly adjoins to the light verb v.

23. Note that what adjoins to T is the complex head V + v. Informally, the adjunction of V + v to T is referred to as *the adjunction of V to T*.

24. See Fukui 1993 and Poole 1994 for related discussion concerning optionality phenomena.

25. The complex heads (resulting from head movement) and their traces are not fully represented when irrelevant.

26. Given that the finite T bears the strong V-feature and attracts V in French, we expect that French should exhibit optional overt object shift in the way Icelandic does, contrary to fact: a parameter yielding this difference is as yet unknown.

27. For a related discussion of the timing of expletive insertion, see Poole 1995.

28. Chomsky (1995, 287) argues that FF[there] has neither Case nor ϕ-features. Consider the following examples:

(i) a. *There seem that [α a lot of people] are intelligent.
    b. *There seem to be [α a man] in the room.

Suppose FF[there] has Case but no ϕ-features in (ia) and checks the Case feature of T but not the ϕ-features of *seem*. Then, FF[α], still bearing ϕ-features (that are

[+interpretable]), raises covertly, checking the φ-features of *seem* and allowing the derivation to converge, contrary to fact. Now suppose FF[there] has φ-features (with [plural]) but no Case feature in (ib) and checks the φ-features of *seem* (with [plural]) but not the Case feature of T. Then, FF[α], still bearing a Case feature (that is [−interpretable]) and the φ-features (with [singular]) (that are [+interpretable]), raises covertly, checking the Case feature of T and allowing the derivation to converge, contrary to fact. Notice that the φ-features of *seem* are checked and erased immediately; hence, the raising of FF[α] (with [singular]) does not induce any feature mismatch. Given the discussion above, Chomsky concludes that FF[there] checks just the strong D-feature of T, so that in (ia), the raising of FF[α] fails to check the Case feature of T, whereas in (ib), the raising of FF[α] induces the feature mismatch between [plural] of *seem* and [singular] of α.

29. For distinct but intimately related proposals on topics connected with expletives, see, among others, Belletti 1988, Chomsky 1986b, 1991, Den Dikken 1995, Groat 1995a, Lasnik 1992, 1995a,b.

30. The answer to (74b) may also explain why the overt application of Move F raises the minimal category α containing FF[F] that allows convergence (Chomsky 1995, 263). Suppose a single application of Erase eliminates any feature F of the head of its target. Then, the overt movement of a larger category β containing α induces additional applications of Erase that eliminate features associated with the distinct heads contained in β (but not in α). Given this, the SDC forces C_{HL} to raise α rather than β (containing α) if the raising of α allows convergence.

31. Chomsky (1995, sec. 4.10) further characterizes the relevant property of T as the toleration of a single unforced violation of Procrastinate. In this appendix, I develop an analysis that dispenses with Procrastinate.

32. Again, the complex heads (resulting from head movement) and their traces are not fully represented when irrelevant.

33. Note that the C-Command Condition permits the use of the outer specifier as an escape hatch in multiple-specifier languages (see, among others, Koizumi 1994, 1995; Ura 1994). For example, consider the mapping in (i), in which WH_2 moves to the outer specifier of C, crossing WH_1 in the inner specifier of C.

(i)

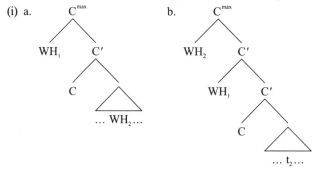

The C-Command Condition prohibits C from attracting WH_1 in (ia); consequently, C attracts WH_2, and WH_2 moves to the outer specifier of C, forming (ib). If some higher C bears a *wh*-feature that must be checked, then the MLC forces WH$_2$ to undergo further *wh*-movement. In such a derivation, WH$_2$ circumvents a *wh*-island violation by using the outer specifier of C as an escape hatch.

34. Chomsky (1995, 372) notes that the same analysis explains the deviance of (i).

(i) *There$_1$ is believed [$_{TP}$ there$_2$ to be someone in the room].

In the LF component, the N-feature of *someone* adjoins to *there$_2$*, and the D-feature of *there$_2$* undergoes erasure. The D-feature of *there$_1$*, however, survives intact to LF, so the derivation of (i) crashes, as desired.

35. I assume with Chomsky (1995) that the trace of an argument chain is inaccessible to C$_{HL}$.

36. Chomsky (1995, 294) proposes that the bare output conditions constrain how the numeration is determined, as stated in (i).

(i) α enters the numeration only if it has an effect on output.

Condition (i) is incorporated into his analysis (in part) to prohibit vacuous movement—for example, the movement of an expletive between the two specifiers of T (inducing no PF effect). But note that such movement, as we have seen, is independently excluded by the C-Command Condition: T fails to c-command its own specifier position; consequently, T cannot attract a category in that position.

Chapter 3

1. Note again that I continue to refer to the operation of movement as Move, though assuming that its correct interpretation is in terms of attraction.

2. In (3), Relativized Minimality is formulated as a constraint on movement. In Rizzi's (1990) proposal, however, Relativized Minimality is formulated as a necessary condition on the relation "antecedent government," given in (i).

(i) X α-governs Y only if there is no Z such that Z is a typical potential α-governor for Y, and Z asymmetrically c-commands Y.

The notion "potential antecedent governor" is then relativized as follows:

(ii) a. Z is a typical potential antecedent governor for Y, Y in an A-chain, iff Z is an A-specifier c-commanding Y.
   b. Z is a typical potential antecedent governor for Y, Y in an Ā-chain, iff Z is an Ā-specifier c-commanding Y.
   c. Z is a typical potential antecedent governor for Y, Y in an X^0-chain, iff Z is a head c-commanding Y.

For detailed discussion of Rizzi's (1990) relativized minimality analysis, see, among others, Chomsky and Lasnik 1993, Frampton 1991.

3. If the nonfinite verb *fix* fails to check the strong feature of C (triggering subject-auxiliary inversion), the derivation of (2a) will never converge because of a violation of the Strong Feature Condition. See Zwart 1993 for relevant discussion of this point.

4. Note that the MLC is not as strong as the HMC (Travis 1984). If the intervening head cannot enter into a checking relation with any sublabel of the target, then such a head may be crossed. The following example, drawn from Southern Tiwa (cited from Allen, Gardiner, and Frantz 1984), is taken to be evidence for such a weaker condition (Baker and Hale 1990):

(i) [DP Yede [NP t1]] a-[seuan]1-mu-ban.
     that   2sS/A-man-see-PAST
     'You saw that man.'

In (i), the noun is incorporated into the verb over the determiner. To allow this head movement (violating the HMC), Baker and Hale (1990) refine Rizzi's (1990) Relativized Minimality to be sensitive to the lexical versus functional distinction. Under the MLC analysis, however, if the determiner cannot enter into a checking relation with any sublabel of the verb, it does not prevent Move from adjoining the noun to the verb (over itself): the noun incorporation in (i) is permitted, as desired.

5. For similar but distinct proposals (incorporating feature relativization), see, among others, Abe 1993, Ferguson 1993, Ferguson and Groat 1994, Kitahara 1994a,b, Ura 1994, 1995.

6. The raising of *him* to the specifier of the matrix T satisfies the MLC but leads the derivation to crash. Notice that the Case feature of the preposition *to*, which is [−interpretable], remains unchecked, thereby surviving intact to LF. For discussion related to Case features of prepositions, see Watanabe 1993 and Ferguson 1994.

7. Chomsky (1995, 272) argues that FF[LI] should have argument (A-position) properties, including the ability to serve as a controller or binder. Consider the following contrast (Lasnik and Saito 1991; Postal 1974):

(i) a. ?The DA proved [TP[α the defendants] to be guilty]
          during [β each other's] trials.
    b. ?*The DA proved [CP that [α the defendants] were guilty]
          during [β each other's] trials.

Suppose the argument properties of α (occupying the embedded subject position) must enter into a c-command relation with β (Condition A). Then, the contrast between (ia) and (ib) shows that in (ia) (but not in (ib)), the argument properties of α enter into a c-command relation with β in the matrix adverbial position. This contrast follows naturally from the LF object shift analysis (Lasnik and Saito 1991). That is, in only the derivation of (ia) does FF[α] covertly adjoin to the matrix verb *proved* for the checking of Case features of *proved* and α; consequently, in the resulting LF representation of (ia), the argument properties of α (included in FF[α]) come to enter into a c-command relation with β in the matrix adverbial position, as desired.

8. This derivational analysis is further supported by examples such as (ia–c) (see, among others, Barss and Lasnik 1986; Ferguson 1994; Jackendoff 1990; Kuno and Takami 1993; Larson 1988, 1990).

(i) a. I talked [$_{PP}$ to [$_α$ the boys]] about [$_β$ themselves].
   b. I received a letter [$_{PP}$ from [$_α$ John]] about [$_β$ him].
   c. I spoke [$_{PP}$ to [$_α$ him]] about [$_β$ Bill's] mother.

In (ia), *themselves* is interpreted as coreferential with *the boys* (Condition A). In (ib), *him* is interpreted as disjoint from *John* (Condition B). In (ic), *Bill* is interpreted as disjoint from *him* (Condition C). The proposed analysis assigns (ia–c) an LF representation resulting from the covert adjunction of FF[α] to the head of the PP (c-commanding β), to which Conditions A, B, and C apply, ensuring the observed interpretations of (ia–c), respectively (and doing so without any reference to an invisible PP node). For further discussion related to the derivational analysis of binding relations, see Epstein et al. 1995 and Kitahara 1996.

9. However, Chomsky (1995, 387 n. 69) points out the unclear status of superiority effects and warns that further detailed investigation is necessary to attain a proper understanding of such effects.

10. It was also proposed that the *Empty Category Principle* (ECP) subsumes the Superiority Condition (see, among others, Aoun, Hornstein, and Sportiche 1981; Huang 1982; Lasnik and Saito 1984). Under this proposal, the LF structures (ia–b) were assigned to (9a–b), given that a *wh*-phrase in situ is adjoined to a *wh*-phrase in Comp at LF to undergo the LF rule of interpretation (Higginbotham and May 1981).

(i) a. I wonder [[what$_2$ who$_1$]$_1$ t$_1$ bought t$_2$]
   b. I wonder [[who$_1$ what$_2$]$_2$ t$_1$ bought t$_2$]

In (ia) (assigned to (9a)), both traces satisfy the ECP: t$_1$ is antecedent-governed and t$_2$ is lexically governed by the verb. In (ib) (assigned to (9b)), however, t$_1$ is neither antecedent-governed nor lexically governed. Thus, the ECP correctly permits (ia) while excluding (ib). The problem for the ECP analysis of superiority effects was posed by pairs such as (iia–b) exhibiting the pure superiority effect (see Hendrick and Rochemont 1982; Pesetsky 1982, 1987).

(ii) a. I wonder [who$_1$ you told t$_1$ [to read what$_2$]].
    b. *I wonder [what$_2$ you told who$_1$ [to read t$_2$]].

Under the ECP analysis, the LF structures (iiia–b) were assigned to (iia–b), respectively.

(iii) a. I wonder [[what$_2$ who$_1$]$_1$ you told t$_1$ [to read t$_2$]]
     b. I wonder [[who$_1$ what$_2$]$_2$ you told t$_1$ [to read t$_2$]]

As shown in (iii), each trace is lexically governed by the verb and the ECP is therefore satisfied: the ECP analysis, unlike the superiority analysis, fails to capture the pure superiority effect.

Pesetsky (1982, 1987) proposes a general condition on movement, which captures both standard and pure superiority effects. He calls it the *Nested Dependency Condition* (NDC).

(iv) *Nested Dependency Condition*
    If two *wh*-trace dependencies overlap, one must contain the other.

He takes *wh*-trace dependencies to be LF chain structures formed by *wh*-movement. Consider the following two LF chain structures:

(v) a.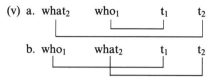

The LF structure (iiia) (assigned the nesting dependency (va)) satisfies the NDC and the movement of *what* is therefore legitimate, whereas the LF structure (iiib) (assigned the intersecting dependency (vb)) violates the NDC and the movement of *who* is therefore illegitimate.

In subsection 3.2.2, I argue that both standard and pure superiority effects are deducible from an independently motivated principle, namely, the MLC: neither the ECP nor the NDC is necessary to capture such effects. See also subsection 3.3.3 for discussion related to other consequences of the NDC.

11. Chomsky (1973, 246) explains his intuition behind the Superiority Condition as follows:

(i) The condition requires that a rule must select the superior term where that rule is ambiguous in application, that is, where the structure given in [(10)] will satisfy the structural condition defining the rule in question with either Z or Y selected as the factor satisfying a given term of this condition. Like the A-over-A Condition, [(10)] restricts the ambiguity of rule application.

Note that his insight that ambiguous rule-application must be restricted in the computational system (i.e., computational complexity must be reduced) is (re)captured in the current formulation of the MLC. For relevant discussion of this point, see also Kitahara 1994a.

12. With regard to a *wh*-phrase in situ in examples such as (9a) and (12a), I assume that such a *wh*-phrase undergoes the LF rule of interpretation with a c-commanding *wh*-phrase occupying the operator position (e.g., the specifier of C) (Higginbotham and May 1981), but it does so without any LF *wh*-movement (Chomsky 1993). Notice further that, under the theory of feature checking (Chomsky 1995), an in-situ *wh*-phrase with a *wh*-feature ([+interpretable]) need not, therefore cannot, undergo *wh*-movement in the LF component. For discussion on topics related to *wh*-phrases in situ, see also Tsai 1994 and Watanabe 1992.

13. See also notes 11 and 12 in chapter 2.

14. In this study, I adopt Huang's (1982) null preposition analysis. But see Murasugi and Saito 1993 for a proposal capturing the argument status of *where* and *when* without postulating the null preposition *p*.

15. For discussion of more complex cases of superiority phenomena, see, among others, Chomsky 1981, 1995, Epstein 1993, Freidin 1995, Kayne 1984, Lasnik and Saito 1992, Oka 1993a,b, Pesetsky 1987, Watanabe 1992.

16. For more recent discussion of PBC phenomena, see Lasnik and Saito 1992, Collins 1994.

17. Since *who* binds no variable in the LF representation resulting from this illegitimate application of Move, the derivation of (19b) crashes because of a violation of the principle of Full Interpretation (FI). See chapter 4 for extensive discussion of the various cases of FI violations.

18. The copy theory of movement is motivated (in part) to capture the absence of the coreference interpretation between *he* and *John* in the following example (Chomsky 1993):

(i) *Which claim that John$_1$ was asleep was he$_1$ willing to discuss?

Given that Condition C of the binding theory applies solely at LF, (i) shows that the complement CP contained in the landing site of the moved *wh*-phrase is interpreted as if it were contained in the departure site of the moved *wh*-phrase. That is, reconstruction is obligatory in (i) (see, among others, Freidin 1986; Lebeaux 1988; Van Riemsdijk and Williams 1981). To explain such a reconstruction effect, Chomsky (1993, 35) proposes the copy theory of movement, under which a trace left by movement is a complete copy of the moved category: literal lowering operations are rendered unnecessary (and now prohibited by the C-Command Condition). Given the copy theory of movement, (i) is assigned the following structure:

(ii) [$_{CP}$ [which claim that John$_1$ was asleep] was [$_{TP}$ he$_1$ willing to discuss t([which claim that John$_1$ was asleep])]]

Chomsky (1993, 41) then proposes the Preference Principle (minimizing the restriction in the operator position, for example, specifier of C). Given this, (ii) is converted (roughly) to the following LF structure:

(iii) [$_{CP}$ (which *x*) was [$_{TP}$ he$_1$ willing to discuss (*x* claim that John$_1$ was asleep)]]

As shown in (iii), the complement CP occurs in the copy position (i.e., the departure site of the moved *wh*-phrase), ensuring a Condition C violation.

Chomsky further argues that reconstruction (i.e., a minimization of the restriction in the operator position) is essentially a reflex of the formation of operator-variable constructions. Thus, reconstruction holds only for operator chains, not for argument chains. This analysis is supported by the following example, in which coreference between *him* and *John* is permitted:

(iv) [$_{\alpha}$ The claim that John$_1$ was asleep] seems to him$_1$ [$_{TP}$ t(α) to be correct].

Given that reconstruction does not hold for the argument chain resulting from the application of Move raising α to the specifier of the matrix T (in the derivation of (iv)), the complement CP in α is interpreted in the specifier of the matrix T, thereby inducing no violation of Condition C. If the complement CP in α were interpreted inside the embedded TP, the coreference interpretation between *John* and *him* would be prohibited, just as in (v) (see also subsection 3.1.3).

(v) *[$_{\alpha}$ They] seem to him$_1$ [$_{TP}$ t(α) to like John$_1$].

For further discussion of reconstruction effects, see Chomsky 1993, 1995, Huang 1993, Takano 1995a.

19. For discussion of the contrast between (21) and (29), see, among others, Browning 1989, Chomsky 1986a, Fiengo et al. 1988, Lasnik and Saito 1992, Tiedeman 1989, Torrego 1985.

20. Following Chomsky (1965) and Epstein (1990), I assume that a descriptively adequate grammar should be able to account for degrees of deviance.

21. Under minimalist assumptions, the derivations of (21) and (29) are not directly generated by the system: the derivation of (21) is generated by relaxing the MLC twice, whereas the derivation of (29) is generated by relaxing the MLC once.

22. An assumption similar to (33) has already been adopted in Chomsky and Lasnik's (1993) analysis of degrees of deviance (involving an illegitimate trace). Assuming that a trace must be properly governed (both antecedent- and head-governed by a lexical feature), Chomsky and Lasnik propose an analysis in which a trace is marked * if it fails either of these conditions, ** if it fails both or if it fails one along with the economy condition, and *** if it fails all three, with multiple starring indicating increased deviance. See also Chomsky 1986a for relevant discussion concerning degrees of deviance.

23. See also Collins and Thráinsson 1993, Fukui and Speas 1986, Kitagawa 1986, Koizumi 1993, 1995, Koopman and Sportiche 1991, and Kuroda 1988.

24. Lasnik and Saito (1992), assuming that the PBC applies at every point of the derivation (the Generalized Proper Binding Condition), propose a control analysis of nondeviant examples such as (44), in which *John* is base-generated outside the embedded predicate that undergoes *wh*-movement; consequently, the derivation of (44) induces no violation of the PBC.

Huang (1993), on the other hand, provides the contrast in (i), supporting the raising analysis of constructions such as (44) (in which *John* is raised from a position inside the embedded predicate).

(i) a. How certain that he$_1$ will win is John$_1$?
    b. How certain to win is John?

Huang notes that the speaker of (ia), in which the embedded pronoun is bound by the matrix subject, presumes "John" to be certain that "John" will win, whereas the speaker of (ib) presumes the addressee to be certain that "John" will win. A unified control analysis of (ia) and (ib) would, by hypothesis, fail to make this distinction between them.

In this study, I adopt the raising analysis of constructions such as (44) and explain why they exhibit no PBC effect. But see Lasnik and Saito 1992 for arguments supporting the control analysis.

25. (53) is adapted from Müller 1993, 1994.

26. But see, among others, Saito 1989, 1992, 1994 and Webelhuth 1989 for empirical arguments suggesting that scrambling is not an instance of morphologically driven movement.

27. I assume that the feature of β that checks the feature triggering short scrambling remains accessible to C_{HL}.

28. In addition, the derivation of (51) yields an LF representation violating FI if the unbound trace t(β) (resulting from these two illegitimate applications of Move) survives to LF and constitutes an illegitimate LF object. In chapter 4, I will extensively discuss topics related to LF objects and FI violations.

29. I assume that H(α), bearing no feature relevant to short scrambling, can be crossed by the short scrambling of β.

30. I assume that β, bearing no feature relevant to topicalization, can be crossed by the topicalization of α.

31. Note that the derivation of German (52) is analogous to the derivation of English (44).

32. For recent proposals concerning long scrambling, see Abe 1993, Kikuchi, Oishi, and Yusa 1994, Kitahara 1994a,b, Miyagawa 1994, Saito 1994, Sakai 1994, Tada 1993, Takano 1995b.

33. Saito (1989, 1992) examines cases such as (i) (which involves one embedding fewer than (64)).

(i) * [$_{CP}$ Mary-ga   t$_1$ yonda-to]$_2$ [sono hon-o]$_1$ John-ga   t$_2$ itta (koto)
       Mary-NOM   read-COMP that book-ACC John-NOM   said (fact)
   'John said that Mary read that book.'
   a. *Long scrambling*
      [sono hon-o]$_1$ John-ga   [$_{CP}$ Mary-ga   t$_1$ yonda-to]$_2$ itta (koto)
      that book-ACC John-NOM   Mary-NOM   read-COMP said (fact)
   b. *Long scrambling*
      [$_{CP}$ Mary-ga   t$_1$ yonda-to]$_2$ [sono hon-o]$_1$ John-ga   t$_2$ itta (koto)
      Mary-NOM   read-COMP that book-ACC John-NOM   said (fact)

In (i), the long scrambling of the embedded object *sono hon-o* 'that book' (see (ia)) precedes the long scrambling of the embedded CP (containing the trace of the scrambled object) (see (ib)). I assume that the scrambling crossing the landing site of the long scrambling is also an instance of long scrambling. Given that the long scrambling crossing the matrix subject is the adjunction to the matrix IP, this analysis of long scrambling incorporates the following assumption:

(ii) In Japanese, ≥ 1 instances of long scrambling can target a projection of the same head (e.g., I).

Saito (1989) presents the following example to support this assumption:

(iii)   [Sono hon-o]$_1$ [Bill-ni]$_2$ John-ga   [$_{CP}$ Mary-ga   kinoo
        that book-ACC Bill-DAT John-NOM   Mary-NOM yesterday
        t$_1$ t$_2$ watasita-to]   omotteiru (koto)
           handed-COMP think   (fact)
   'John thinks that Mary handed that book to Bill yesterday.'
   a. *Long scrambling*
      [Bill-ni]$_2$ John-ga   [$_{CP}$ Mary-ga   kinoo   [sono hon-o]$_1$ t$_2$
      Bill-DAT John-NOM   Mary-NOM yesterday that book-ACC
      watasita-to]   omotteiru (koto)
      handed-COMP think   (fact)

b. *Long scrambling*
   [sono hon-o]₁ [Bill-ni]₂ John-ga [CP Mary-ga kinoo   t₁ t₂
   that book-ACC Bill-DAT John-NOM   Mary-NOM yesterday
   watasita-to] omotteiru (koto)
   handed-COMP think   (fact)

In (iii), there are two instances of long scrambling (targeting a projection of the matrix I): the long scrambling of the embedded indirect object *Bill-ni* 'to Bill' and the long scrambling of the embedded direct object *sono hon-o* 'that book'.

This multiple-scrambling analysis, however, is confronted with the following contrast:

(iv) a. *[Gatugatu]₂ John-ga [CP Mary-ga [sushi-o]₁ t₂ tabeta-to]
        greedily   John-NOM   Mary-NOM sushi-ACC   ate-COMP
        itta (koto)
        said (fact)
        'John said that Mary ate sushi greedily.'
    b. [Sushi-o]₁ [gatugatu]₂ John-ga [CP Mary-ga t₁ t₂ tabeta-to]
       sushi-ACC greedily   John-NOM   Mary-NOM   ate-COMP
       itta (koto)
       said (fact)

As noted in the literature, the long scrambling of adverbial expressions such as *gatugatu* 'greedily' results in deviance (see (iva)). Suppose the adverbial expression *gatugatu* is prohibited from undergoing long scrambling. Then, the derivation of (ivb), involving two instances of long scrambling (namely, the long scrambling of the embedded object and the long scrambling of the embedded manner adverb) should exhibit deviance because of the instance of long scrambling that raises *gatugatu* 'greedily'; but it does not.

The absence of deviance in (ivb) receives a natural explanation if the derivation of (ivb) employs only one instance of long scrambling that raises a category containing both the embedded object and the embedded manner adverb (Koizumi 1991, 1995). That is, C_{HL} employs one application of Move raising some larger category γ that contains both the embedded object and the embedded manner adverb, yielding (v).

(v) [γ[sushi-o]₁ [gatugatu]₂] John-ga   [CP Mary-ga t(γ) tabeta-to] itta (koto)
    sushi-ACC greedily   John-NOM   Mary-NOM   ate-COMP said (fact)

γ can be some verbal projection if the Japanese finite verb undergoes overt verb movement (Koizumi 1991, 1995; Otani and Whitman 1991; Whitman 1991).

The same analysis holds for the following contrast:

(vi) a. *[Kinoo]₁ John-ga [CP Mary-ga t₁ [sono hon-o]₂ [Bill-ni]₃
        yesterday John-NOM   Mary-NOM   that book-ACC Bill-DAT
        watasita-to] omotteiru (koto)
        handed-COMP think   (fact)
        'John thinks that Mary handed that book to Bill yesterday.'
     b. [Kinoo]₁ [sono hon-o]₂ [Bill-ni]₃ John-ga [CP Mary-ga t₁ t₂ t₃
        yesterday that book   Bill-DAT John-NOM   Mary-NOM
        watasita-to] omotteiru (koto)
        handed-COMP think   (fact)

Given that temporal adverbials such as *kinoo* 'yesterday' are prohibited from undergoing long scrambling (see (via)), the nondeviant (vib) is (presumably) assigned the following structure:

(vii) [γ [kinoo]₁   [sono hon-o]₂   [Bill-ni]₃] John-ga [CP Mary-ga   t(γ)
           yesterday   that book-ACC Bill-DAT John-NOM   Mary-NOM
     watasita-to]   omotteiru (koto)
     handed-COMP think   (fact)

Now notice that this single-scrambling analysis undermines (iii) as evidence supporting assumption (ii), since the following structure, which results from a single instance of long scrambling, can also be assigned to (iii):

(viii) [γ [sono hon-o]₁   [Bill-ni]₂] John-ga [CP Mary-ga   kinoo   t(γ)
            that book-ACC Bill-DAT John-NOM   Mary-NOM yesterday
      watasita-to]   omotteiru (koto)
      handed-COMP think   (fact)

Suppose the central cases motivating assumption (ii) (e.g., (iii)) can be explained without invoking multiple instances of long scrambling. Then, the question arises whether assumption (ii) is necessary. If, contrary to this assumption, at most one instance of long scrambling can target a projection of the head (e.g., I) in Japanese, the structure of (i) to which Spell-Out applies cannot be generated in the first place.

To avoid any potential problem related to assumption (ii), I limit the discussion to cases such as (64), the derivation of which involves two separate heads projecting targets for multiple instances of long scrambling.

34. I assume that the feature of β that checks the feature triggering long scrambling remains accessible to C_{HL}.

35. Note that the derivation of Japanese (64) is analogous to the derivation of English (21).

Chapter 4

1. Argument versus adjunct asymmetries such as the one in (1) have long occupied the center of syntactic investigation. For detailed discussion of such asymmetries, see, among others, Chomsky 1981, 1986a, Chomsky and Lasnik 1993, Cinque 1990, Epstein 1987, 1991, Huang 1982, Kayne 1984, Lasnik and Saito 1984, 1992, Manzini 1992, Oishi 1993, Rizzi 1990.

2. Following Chomsky (1995, 289), I assume that *whether* inserted in the checking domain of C_{wh} (bearing a *wh*-feature) occupies the specifier of C_{wh}. Also note that the *wh*-feature of *whether* is [+interpretable]; hence, it is accessible to C_{HL} throughout, whether checked or not.

3. Chomsky and Lasnik (1993), following Lasnik and Saito (1984, 1992), argue that the derivation of (1a), unlike the derivation of (1b), induces a violation of FI at LF. Under their analysis, traces created by *wh*-island extraction are uniformly marked * upon their creation, and t* is an offending trace (inducing a violation of FI at LF). Assuming that long-distance *wh*-movement first adjoins an embedded

wh-category to the embedded VP, then moves it to the specifier of the matrix C, crossing the *wh*-island, Chomsky and Lasnik assign the following structures to (1a–b), respectively:

(i) a. [$_{CP}$ how$_1$ do you wonder [$_{CP}$ whether John [$_{VP}$ t$_1'$* [$_{VP}$ fixed the car t$_1$]]]]
   b. [$_{CP}$ what$_1$ do you wonder [$_{CP}$ whether John [$_{VP}$ t$_1'$* [$_{VP}$ fixed t$_1$]]]]

In each derivation, the second application of successive-cyclic *wh*-movement crosses the *wh*-island, thereby leaving a *-marked trace behind. Chomsky and Lasnik assume that the creation of such a *-marked trace yields marginal deviance (a Subjacency effect). To capture the greater degree of deviance exhibited by (1a), they incorporate the following general condition, which we might call the *Trace Deletion Condition* (TDC) (adapted from the condition on the uniformity of chains—see Browning 1987, Chomsky and Lasnik 1993).

(ii) *Trace Deletion Condition*
   An intermediate trace of the operator chain CH deletes if CH terminates in an A-position.

The TDC converts the structures (ia–b) to the LF structures (iiia–b), respectively.

(iii) a. [$_{CP}$ how$_1$ do you wonder [$_{CP}$ whether John [$_{VP}$ t$_1'$* [$_{VP}$ fixed the car t$_1$]]]]
   b. [$_{CP}$ what$_1$ do you wonder [$_{CP}$ whether John [$_{VP}$ $\emptyset$ [$_{VP}$ fixed t$_1$]]]]

Given the TDC, the offending trace of the chain CH (how$_1$, t$_1'$*, t$_1$) (headed by *how* and terminating in an Ā-position) remains unaffected, yielding (iiia), whereas the offending trace of the chain CH (what$_1$, t$_1'$*, t$_1$) (headed by *what* and terminating in an A-position) undergoes deletion, yielding (iiib). Assuming that a chain with an offending trace is not a legitimate LF object, Chomsky and Lasnik argue that the derivation of (1a) (yielding the LF representation (iiia)) induces an additional violation, namely, a violation of FI at LF (an ECP effect), whereas the derivation of (1b) (yielding the LF representation (iiib)) induces no violation of FI at LF but still exhibits marginal deviance because the *wh*-island extraction has created a *-marked trace (a Subjacency effect).

Therefore, Chomsky and Lasnik's (1993) analysis captures the contrast exhibited by (1a–b) by appealing to the *-marking algorithm and the TDC.

Following their insights, I construct a general theory of chain formation on independent grounds (see section 4.2), under which I demonstrate that the empirically desirable aspects of the *-marking algorithm and the TDC can be explained by appealing to an already existing, independently motivated Case-theoretic distinction (see sections 4.3 and 4.4).

4. Note that Chomsky and Lasnik's (1993) analysis fails to capture the contrast in (5) if both *what* and *how many pounds* are base-generated in the complement of the verb *weigh* (an A-position).

5. Rizzi (1990), taking the contrast in (5) to be a referential versus nonreferential asymmetry, suggests that objects (e.g., *what*), unlike quasi objects (e.g., *how many pounds*), are assigned referential indices (or certain θ-roles), and only those categories with referential indices can yield legitimate chains across islands. See Frampton 1991 for a detailed and insightful discussion of Rizzi's (1990) relativized minimality analysis. For a very similar indexing analysis, see Epstein 1987, 1991.

6. The class of LF chains also includes other chains such as a head chain, and arguably a predicate chain.

7. Given that an argument chain terminates with an element in a θ-marked position (see (8a)), the pair (FF[α], t(FF[α])) is not an argument chain. Notice that t(FF[α]) is part of the head of t(α), t(α) a complement of the verb *fix*. What counts as the argument chain headed by FF[α] in the LF representation of (15) is the pair (FF[α], t(α)) terminating with t(α) in a θ-marked position.

8. The SFC still ensures the checking of strong features before Spell-Out applies. Note that Chomsky's (1995) version of the SFC (stipulating that overt movement is cyclic) excludes the noncyclic derivation of (25).

9. Note that (31) is still weaker than Chomsky's (1995) version of the SFC, which directly incorporates the "strict cyclicity" property of overt movement.

10. Note that the contrast in (32) has resisted a principled account under the framework of Chomsky 1995 (incorporating the strong version of the SFC).

11. Note that the cyclic derivation of (32b), just like the cyclic derivation of (32a), crashes; hence, the cyclic derivation of (32b) does not block its noncyclic counterpart, namely, the convergent derivation of (32b) examined here.

12. Recall that an argument chain is headed by an element in a Case-checking position and terminates with an element in a θ-marked position (see (8a)).

13. Note that this Case-theoretic analysis crucially rests on the assumption that the verb *weigh* has no Case feature when it takes a Caseless quasi object as its complement.

14. The Case-theoretic distinction between quasi objects and objects was discussed by Noam Chomsky (class lectures, fall 1989).

15. See note 14 in chapter 3.

16. The contrast between (53) and (56) is attributed to Adriana Belletti (see Chomsky 1982, 1986a).

17. See note 30 in chapter 2.

18. I leave for future research the task of determining what property permits the smallest category containing the *wh*-feature of *whom* to expand from the prepositional complement *whom* (see the derivation of (57a)) to the verbal complement *to whom* (see the derivation of (57b)).

19. Note that the nonconvergent derivation of (56) (taking the verbal complement *to whom* to be the smallest category containing FF[whom] and raising *to whom*) is analogous to the nonconvergent derivations of (47a–b).

References

Abe, Jun. 1993. Binding conditions and scrambling without A/A' distinction. Doctoral dissertation, University of Connecticut, Storrs.

Abe, Jun. 1996. What triggers successive-cyclic movement. Ms., Toyo Women's College, Chiba, Japan.

Allen, Barbara J., Donna B. Gardiner, and Donald G. Frantz. 1984. Noun incorporation in Southern Tiwa. *IJAL* 50, 292–311.

Aoun, Joseph, Norbert Hornstein, and Dominique Sportiche. 1981. On some aspects of wide scope quantification. *Journal of Linguistic Research* 1.3, 67–95.

Baker, Mark, and Kenneth Hale. 1990. Relativized Minimality and pronoun incorporation. *Linguistic Inquiry* 21, 289–297.

Barss, Andrew, and Howard Lasnik. 1986. A note on anaphora and double objects. *Linguistic Inquiry* 17, 347–354.

Belletti, Adriana. 1988. The Case of unaccusatives. *Linguistic Inquiry* 19, 1–34.

Belletti, Adriana. 1990. *Generalized verb movement*. Turin: Rosenberg & Sellier.

Besten, Hans den, and Gert Webelhuth. 1990. Stranding. In *Scrambling and barriers*, eds. Günther Grewendorf and Wolfgang Sternefeld, 77–92. Amsterdam: John Benjamins.

Bobaljik, Jonathan. 1995. In terms of merger: Single output syntax and the strict cycle. In *MIT working papers in linguistics 27: Papers on minimalist syntax*, 41–64. MITWPL, Department of Linguistics and Philosophy, MIT, Cambridge, Mass.

Bošković, Željko. 1993. On certain violations of the Superiority Condition, AgrO, and economy of derivation. Ms., University of Connecticut, Storrs.

Brody, Michael. 1993. θ-theory and arguments. *Linguistic Inquiry* 24, 1–23.

Brody, Michael. 1995. *Lexico-Logical Form: A radically minimalist theory*. Cambridge, Mass.: MIT Press.

Browning, M. A. 1987. Null operator constructions. Doctoral dissertation, MIT, Cambridge, Mass.

Browning, M. A. 1989. ECP ≠ CED. *Linguistic Inquiry* 20, 481–491.

Browning, M. A. 1991. Bounding conditions on representation. *Linguistic Inquiry* 22, 541–562.

Chomsky, Noam. 1955. The logical structure of linguistic theory. Ms., Harvard University, Cambridge, Mass. [Revised 1956 version published in part by Plenum, 1975; University of Chicago Press, 1985.]

Chomsky, Noam. 1965. *Aspects of the theory of syntax.* Cambridge, Mass.: MIT Press.

Chomsky, Noam. 1973. Conditions on transformations. In *A festschrift for Morris Halle*, eds. Stephen R. Anderson and Paul Kiparsky, 232–286. New York: Holt, Rinehart and Winston.

Chomsky, Noam. 1981. *Lectures on government and binding.* Dordrecht: Foris.

Chomsky, Noam. 1982. *Some concepts and consequences of the theory of government and binding.* Cambridge, Mass.: MIT Press.

Chomsky, Noam. 1986a. *Barriers.* Cambridge, Mass.: MIT Press.

Chomsky, Noam. 1986b. *Knowledge of language: Its nature, origin, and use.* New York: Praeger.

Chomsky, Noam. 1991. Some notes on economy of derivation and representation. In *Principles and parameters in comparative grammar*, ed. Robert Freidin, 417–454. Cambridge, Mass.: MIT Press. [Reprinted in *The Minimalist Program*, 129–166. Cambridge, Mass.: MIT Press, 1995.]

Chomsky, Noam. 1993. A minimalist program for linguistic theory. In *The view from Building 20: Essays in linguistics in honor of Sylvain Bromberger*, eds. Kenneth Hale and Samuel Jay Keyser, 1–52. Cambridge, Mass.: MIT Press. [Reprinted in *The Minimalist Program*, 167–217. Cambridge, Mass.: MIT Press, 1995.]

Chomsky, Noam. 1994. Bare phrase structure. MIT Occasional Papers in Linguistics 5. MITWPL, Department of Linguistics and Philosophy, MIT, Cambridge, Mass. [Published in *Evolution and revolution in linguistic theory: Essays in honor of Carlos Otero*, eds. Héctor Campos and Paula Kempchinsky, 51–109. Washington, D.C.: Georgetown University Press, 1995. Also published in *Government and Binding Theory and the Minimalist Program*, ed. Gert Webelhuth, 383–439. Oxford: Blackwell, 1995.]

Chomsky, Noam. 1995. Categories and transformations. In *The Minimalist Program*, 219–394. Cambridge, Mass.: MIT Press.

Chomsky, Noam, and Howard Lasnik. 1993. The theory of principles and parameters. In *Syntax: An international handbook of contemporary research*, eds. Joachim Jacobs, Arnim von Stechow, Wolfgang Sternefeld, and Theo Vennemann, 506–569. Berlin: Walter de Gruyter. [Reprinted in *The Minimalist Program*, 13–127. Cambridge, Mass.: MIT Press, 1995.]

Cinque, Guglielmo. 1990. *Types of Ā-dependencies.* Cambridge, Mass.: MIT Press.

Collins, Chris. 1994. Economy of derivation and the Generalized Proper Binding Condition. *Linguistic Inquiry* 25, 45–61.

Collins, Chris. 1995. Toward a theory of optimal derivations. In *MIT working papers in linguistics 27: Papers on minimalist syntax*, 65–103. MITWPL, Department of Linguistics and Philosophy, MIT, Cambridge, Mass.

Collins, Chris, and Höskuldur Thráinsson. 1993. Object shift in double object constructions and the theory of Case. In *MIT working papers in linguistics 19: Papers on Case & agreement II*, 131–174. MITWPL, Department of Linguistics and Philosophy, MIT, Cambridge, Mass.

Diesing, Molly. 1992. *Indefinites.* Cambridge, Mass.: MIT Press.

Dikken, Marcel den. 1995. Binding, expletives, and levels. *Linguistic Inquiry* 26, 347–354.

Emonds, Joseph. 1978. The verbal complex V′ − V in French. *Linguistic Inquiry* 9, 49–77.

Epstein, Samuel D. 1987. Empty categories and their antecedents. Doctoral dissertation, University of Connecticut, Storrs.

Epstein, Samuel D. 1990. Differentiation and reduction in syntactic theory: A case study. *Natural Language & Linguistic Theory* 8, 313–323.

Epstein, Samuel D. 1991. *Traces and their antecedents.* New York: Oxford University Press.

Epstein, Samuel D. 1992. Derivational constraints on Ā-chain formation. *Linguistic Inquiry* 23, 135–159.

Epstein, Samuel D. 1993. Superiority. In *Harvard working papers in linguistics 3*, 14–64. Department of Linguistics, Harvard University, Cambridge, Mass.

Epstein, Samuel D. 1994. The derivation of syntactic relations. Ms., Harvard University, Cambridge, Mass. [Paper presented at the Harvard University Linguistics Department Forum in Synchronic Linguistic Theory, December 1994.]

Epstein, Samuel D. 1995. Un-principled syntax and the derivation of syntactic relations. Ms., Harvard University, Cambridge, Mass.

Epstein, Samuel D., Erich Groat, Ruriko Kawashima, and Hisatsugu Kitahara. 1995. Non-representational syntax: A derivational approach to syntactic relations. Ms., Harvard University, Cambridge, Mass., and the University of British Columbia, Vancouver. [To appear, Oxford University Press.]

Ferguson, Scott K. 1993. Notes on the shortest move metric and object checking. In *Harvard working papers in linguistics 3*, 65–80. Department of Linguistics, Harvard University, Cambridge, Mass.

Ferguson, Scott K. 1994. Deriving the invisibility of PP nodes for command from $AGR^0 + P^0$ Case checking. In *Harvard working papers in linguistics 4*, 30–36. Department of Linguistics, Harvard University, Cambridge, Mass.

Ferguson, Scott K., and Erich Groat. 1994. Defining "shortest move." Ms., Harvard University, Cambridge, Mass. [Paper presented at the 17th GLOW Colloquium.]

Fiengo, Robert. 1977. On trace theory. *Linguistic Inquiry* 8, 35–61.

Fiengo, Robert, C.-T. James Huang, Howard Lasnik, and Tanya Reinhart. 1988. The syntax of *wh*-in-situ. In *Proceedings of the Seventh West Coast Conference on Formal Linguistics*, 81–98. Stanford, Calif.: CSLI Publications. [Distributed by Cambridge University Press.]

Frampton, John. 1991. *Relativized Minimality*: A review. *The Linguistic Review* 8, 1–46.

Freidin, Robert. 1978. Cyclicity and the theory of grammar. *Linguistic Inquiry* 9, 519–549.

Freidin, Robert. 1986. Fundamental issues in the theory of binding. In *Studies in the acquisition of anaphora*, vol. 1, ed. Barbara Lust, 151–188. Dordrecht: Reidel.

Freidin, Robert. 1992. *Foundations of generative syntax*. Cambridge, Mass.: MIT Press.

Freidin, Robert. 1995. Superiority, subjacency, and economy. In *Evolution and revolution in linguistic theory: Essays in honor of Carlos Otero*, eds. Héctor Campos and Paula Kempchinsky, 138–167. Washington, D.C.: Georgetown University Press.

Fukui, Naoki. 1993. Parameters and optionality. *Linguistic Inquiry* 24, 399–420.

Fukui, Naoki, and Margaret Speas. 1986. Specifiers and projections. In *MIT working papers in linguistics 8: Papers in theoretical linguistics*, 128–172. MITWPL, Department of Linguistics and Philosophy, MIT, Cambridge, Mass.

Grewendorf, Günther, and Joachim Sabel. 1994. Long scrambling and incorporation. *Linguistic Inquiry* 25, 263–308.

Groat, Erich. 1995a. English expletives: A minimalist approach. *Linguistic Inquiry* 26, 354–365.

Groat, Erich. 1995b. On the redundancy of syntactic representations. Ms., Harvard University, Cambridge, Mass. [Paper presented at the 18th GLOW Colloquium.]

Haig, John. 1976. Shadow pronoun deletion in Japanese. *Linguistic Inquiry* 7, 363–371.

Hale, Kenneth, and Samuel Jay Keyser. 1993. On argument structure and the lexical expression of syntactic relations. In *The view from Building 20: Essays in linguistics in honor of Sylvain Bromberger*, eds. Kenneth Hale and Samuel Jay Keyser, 53–109. Cambridge, Mass.: MIT Press.

Harada, Shin-Ichi. 1977. Nihongo ni henkei wa hituyoo da. *Gengo* 6.10, 88–95; 6.11, 96–103.

Hendrick, Randall, and Michael Rochemont. 1982. Complementation, multiple *wh*, and echo questions. Ms., University of North Carolina at Chapel Hill and University of California at Irvine.

Higginbotham, James, and Robert May. 1981. Questions, quantifiers, and crossing. *The Linguistic Review* 1, 41–80.

Holmberg, Anders. 1986. Word order and syntactic features in the Scandinavian languages and English. Doctoral dissertation, University of Stockholm.

Huang, C.-T. James. 1982. Logical relations in Chinese and the theory of grammar. Doctoral dissertation, MIT, Cambridge, Mass.

Huang, C.-T. James. 1993. Reconstruction and the structure of VP: Some theoretical consequences. *Linguistic Inquiry* 24, 103–138.

Iatridou, Sabine. 1990. About Agr(P). *Linguistic Inquiry* 21, 551–577.

Jackendoff, Ray. 1977. *X̄ syntax: A study of phrase structure.* Cambridge, Mass.: MIT Press.

Jackendoff, Ray. 1990. On Larson's treatment of the double object construction. *Linguistic Inquiry* 21, 427–456.

Jonas, Dianne. 1992. Case theory and nominative case in Icelandic. In *Harvard working papers in linguistics* 1, 175–195. Department of Linguistics, Harvard University, Cambridge, Mass.

Jonas, Dianne. 1995. Clause structure and verb syntax in Scandinavian and English. Doctoral dissertation, Harvard University, Cambridge, Mass.

Jonas, Dianne. 1996. Clause structure, expletives and verb movement. In *Minimal ideas*: Syntactic Studies in the Minimalist Framework, eds. Werner Abraham, Samuel D. Epstein, Höskuldur Thránsson, and C. Jan-Wouter Zwart, 167–188. Amsterdam: John Benjamins.

Jonas, Dianne, and Jonathan David Bobaljik. 1993. Specs for subjects: The role of TP in Icelandic. In *MIT working papers in linguistics 18: Papers on Case & agreement I*, 59–98. MITWPL, Department of Linguistics and Philosophy, MIT, Cambridge, Mass.

Kawashima, Ruriko. 1994. The structure of noun phrases and the interpretation of quantificational NPs in Japanese. Doctoral dissertation, Cornell University, Ithaca, N.Y.

Kawashima, Ruriko, and Hisatsugu Kitahara. 1996. Strict cyclicity, linear ordering, and derivational c-command. In *Proceedings of the Fourteenth West Coast Conference on Formal Linguistics*, 255–269. Stanford, Calif.: CSLI Publications. [Distributed by Cambridge University Press.]

Kayne, Richard. 1984. *Connectedness and binary branching.* Dordrecht.: Foris.

Kayne, Richard. 1993. The antisymmetry of syntax. Ms., Graduate Center, CUNY, New York.

Kayne, Richard. 1994. *The antisymmetry of syntax.* Cambridge, Mass.: MIT Press.

Kikuchi, Akira, Masayuki Oishi, and Noriaki Yusa. 1994. Scrambling and relativized L-relatedness. In *MIT working papers in linguistics 24: Formal Approaches to Japanese Linguistics (FAJL) 1*, 141–158. MITWPL, Department of Linguistics and Philosophy, MIT, Cambridge, Mass.

Kitagawa, Yoshihisa. 1986. Subject in Japanese and English. Doctoral dissertation, University of Massachusetts, Amherst.

Kitahara, Hisatsugu. 1994a. Restricting ambiguous rule-application: A unified analysis of movement. In *MIT working papers in linguistics 24: Formal Approaches to Japanese Linguistics (FAJL) 1*, 179–209. MITWPL, Department of Linguistics and Philosophy, MIT, Cambridge, Mass.

Kitahara, Hisatsugu. 1994b. Target α: A unified theory of movement and structure-building. Doctoral dissertation, Harvard University, Cambridge, Mass.

Kitahara, Hisatsugu. 1995. Target α: Deducing strict cyclicity from derivational economy. *Linguistic Inquiry* 26, 47–77.

Kitahara, Hisatsugu. 1996. A derivational solution to conflicting c-command relations. Ms., University of British Columbia, Vancouver.

Koizumi, Masatoshi. 1991. Modal phrase and types of movements. Ms., MIT, Cambridge, Mass. [Paper presented at Japanese/Korean Linguistics 2.]

Koizumi, Masatoshi. 1993. Object agreement phrases and the split VP hypothesis. In *MIT working papers in linguistics 18: Papers on Case & agreement I*, 99–148. MITWPL, Department of Linguistics and Philosophy, MIT, Cambridge, Mass.

Koizumi, Masatoshi. 1994. Layered specifiers. In *NELS 24*, 255–269. GLSA, University of Massachusetts, Amherst.

Koizumi, Masatoshi. 1995. Phrase structure in minimalist syntax. Doctoral dissertation, MIT, Cambridge, Mass.

Koopman, Hilda, and Dominique Sportiche. 1991. The position of subjects. *Lingua* 85, 211–258.

Kuno, Susumu, and Ken-ichi Takami. 1993. *Grammar and discourse principles: Functional syntax and GB Theory*. Chicago: University of Chicago Press.

Kuroda, S.-Y. 1988. Whether we agree or not: A comparative syntax of English and Japanese. *Lingvisticae Investigationes* 12, 1–47.

Larson, Richard. 1988. On the double object construction. *Linguistic Inquiry* 19, 335–391.

Larson, Richard. 1990. Double objects revisited: Reply to Jackendoff. *Linguistic Inquiry* 21, 589–632.

Lasnik, Howard. 1992. Case and expletives: Notes toward a parametric account. *Linguistic Inquiry* 23, 381–405.

Lasnik, Howard. 1995a. Case and expletives revisited: On Greed and other human failings. *Linguistic Inquiry* 26, 615–633.

Lasnik, Howard. 1995b. Last Resort. In *Minimalism and linguistic theory*, eds. Shosuke Haraguchi and Michio Funaki, 1–32. Tokyo: Hituzi Shyobo.

Lasnik, Howard, and Mamoru Saito. 1984. On the nature of proper government. *Linguistic Inquiry* 15, 235–289.

Lasnik, Howard, and Mamoru Saito. 1991. On the subject of infinitives. In *CLS 27*. Vol. 1, 324–343. Chicago Linguistic Society, University of Chicago, Chicago, Ill.

Lasnik, Howard, and Mamoru Saito. 1992. *Move α: Conditions on its application and output*. Cambridge, Mass.: MIT Press.

Lebeaux, David. 1988. Language acquisition and the form of grammar. Doctoral dissertation, University of Massachusetts, Amherst.

Longobardi, Giuseppe. 1994. Reference and proper names. *Linguistic Inquiry* 25, 609–665.

Mahajan, Anoop. 1990. The A/A-bar distinction and movement theory. Doctoral dissertation, MIT, Cambridge, Mass.

Manzini, M. Rita. 1992. *Locality: A theory and some of its empirical consequences.* Cambridge, Mass.: MIT Press.

May, Robert. 1977. The grammar of quantification. Doctoral dissertation, MIT, Cambridge, Mass.

May, Robert. 1985. *Logical Form.* Cambridge, Mass.: MIT Press.

Miyagawa, Shigeru. 1994. Nonconfigurationality within a configurational structure. Ms., MIT, Cambridge, Mass.

Müller, Gereon. 1993. On deriving movement type asymmetries. Doctoral dissertation, Universität Tübingen.

Müller, Gereon. 1994. A constraint on remnant movement. Ms., Universität Tübingen.

Müller, Gereon, and Wolfgang Sternefeld. 1993. Improper movement and unambiguous binding. *Linguistic Inquiry* 24, 461–507.

Murasugi, Keiko, and Mamoru Saito. 1993. Quasi-adjuncts as sentential arguments. In *Proceedings of the Western Conference on Linguistics 5*, 251–264. Department of Linguistics, California State University, Fresno.

Muysken, Pieter. 1982. Parameterizing the notion "head." *Journal of Linguistic Research* 2, 57–75.

Nuñes, Jairo. 1995. On why traces cannot be phonetically realized. Ms., University of Maryland, College Park/University of Southern California, Los Angeles. [Paper presented at NELS 26.]

Oishi, Masayuki. 1990. Conceptual problems of upward X-bar theory. Ms., Tohoku Gakuin University, Sendai, Japan. [Truncated version published in *Explorations in generative grammar: A festschrift for Dong-Whee Yang*, eds. Young-Sun Kim, Kyoung-Jae Lee, Byung-Choon Lee, Hyun-Kwon Yang, and Jong-Yurl Yoon, 455–490. Seoul: Hankuk, 1994.]

Oishi, Masayuki. 1993. LF legitimacy and chain formation. Ms., Tohoku Gakuin University, Sendai, Japan.

Oka, Toshifusa. 1993a. Minimalism in syntactic derivation. Doctoral dissertation, MIT, Cambridge, Mass.

Oka, Toshifusa. 1993b. Shallowness. In *MIT working papers in linguistics 19: Papers on Case & agreement II*, 255–320. MITWPL, Department of Linguistics and Philosophy, MIT, Cambridge, Mass.

Otani, Kazuyo, and John Whitman. 1991. V-raising and VP-ellipsis. *Linguistic Inquiry* 22, 345–358.

Pesetsky, David. 1982. Paths and categories. Doctoral dissertation, MIT, Cambridge, Mass.

Pesetsky, David. 1987. *Wh*-in-situ: Movement and unselective binding. In *The representation of (in)definiteness*, eds. Eric J. Reuland and Alice G. B. ter Meulen, 98–129. Cambridge, Mass.: MIT Press.

Pollock, Jean-Yves. 1989. Verb movement, Universal Grammar, and the structure of IP. *Linguistic Inquiry* 20, 365–424.

Poole, Geoffrey. 1994. Optional movement in the Minimalist Program. Ms., Harvard University, Cambridge, Mass.

Poole, Geoffrey. 1995. Constraints on local economy. Ms., Harvard University, Cambridge, Mass. [To appear in *Is the Best Good Enough?*, eds. Pilar Barbosa, Danny Fox, Paul Hagstrom, Martha McGinnis, and David Pesetsky. Cambridge, Mass.: MIT Press.]

Postal, Paul M. 1974. *On raising.* Cambridge, Mass.: MIT Press.

Reinhart, Tanya. 1976. The syntactic domain of anaphora. Doctoral dissertation, MIT, Cambridge, Mass.

Riemsdijk, Henk van, and Edwin Williams. 1981. NP-Structure. *The Linguistic Review* 1, 171–218.

Rizzi, Luigi. 1990. *Relativized Minimality.* Cambridge, Mass.: MIT Press.

Ross, John Robert. 1967. Constraints on variables in syntax. Doctoral dissertation, MIT, Cambridge, Mass.

Saito, Mamoru. 1985. Some asymmetries in Japanese and their theoretical implications. Doctoral dissertation, MIT, Cambridge, Mass.

Saito, Mamoru. 1989. Scrambling as semantically vacuous A'-movement. In *Alternative conceptions of phrase structure*, eds. Mark Baltin and Anthony Kroch, 182–200. Chicago: University of Chicago Press.

Saito, Mamoru. 1992. Long distance scrambling in Japanese. *Journal of East Asian Linguistics* 1, 69–118.

Saito, Mamoru. 1994. Improper adjunction. In *MIT working papers in linguistics 24: Formal Approaches to Japanese Linguistics (FAJL) 1*, 263–293. MITWPL, Department of Linguistics and Philosophy, MIT, Cambridge, Mass.

Sakai, Hiromu. 1994. Derivational economy in long distance scrambling. In *MIT working papers in linguistics 24: Formal Approaches to Japanese Linguistics (FAJL) 1*, 295–314. MITWPL, Department of Linguistics and Philosophy, MIT, Cambridge, Mass.

Speas, Margaret J. 1986. Adjunction and projection in syntax. Doctoral dissertation, MIT, Cambridge, Mass.

Speas, Margaret J. 1990. *Phrase structure in natural language.* Dordrecht: Kluwer.

Stowell, Tim. 1981. Origins of phrase structure. Doctoral dissertation, MIT, Cambridge, Mass.

Tada, Hiroaki. 1993. A/A-bar partition in derivation. Doctoral dissertation, MIT, Cambridge, Mass.

Takahashi, Daiko. 1994. Minimality of movement. Doctoral dissertation, University of Connecticut, Storrs.

Takano, Yuji. 1995a. Predicate fronting and internal subjects. *Linguistic Inquiry* 26, 327–340.

Takano, Yuji. 1995b. Scrambling, relativized minimality, and economy of derivation. In *Proceedings of the Thirteenth West Coast Conference on Formal Linguistics*, 385–399. Stanford, Calif.: CSLI Publications. [Distributed by Cambridge University Press.]

Thráinsson, Höskuldur. 1993. On the structure of infinitival complements. In *Harvard working papers in linguistics 3*, 181–213. Department of Linguistics, Harvard University, Cambridge, Mass.

Tiedeman, Robyne C. 1989. Government and locality conditions on syntactic relations. Doctoral dissertation, University of Connecticut, Storrs.

Torrego, Esther. 1984. On inversion in Spanish and some of its effects. *Linguistic Inquiry* 15, 103–129.

Torrego, Esther. 1985. On empty categories in nominals. Ms., University of Massachusetts, Boston.

Toyoshima, Takashi. 1996. Derivational CED: A consequence of the bottom-up parallel-process of Merge and Attract. Ms., Cornell University, Ithaca, N.Y. [To appear in *Proceedings of the Fifteenth West Coast Conference on Formal Linguistics*. Stanford, Calif.: CSLI Publications.]

Travis, Lisa. 1984. Parameters and effects of word order variation. Doctoral dissertation, MIT, Cambridge, Mass.

Tsai, Wei-Tien Dylan. 1994. On economizing the theory of A′-dependencies. Doctoral dissertation, MIT, Cambridge, Mass.

Ura, Hiroyuki. 1994. Varieties of raising and the feature-based phrase structure theory. MIT Occasional Papers in Linguistics 7. MITWPL, Department of Linguistics and Philosophy, MIT, Cambridge, Mass.

Ura, Hiroyuki. 1995. Towards a "strictly derivational" economy condition. In *MIT working papers in linguistics 27: Papers on minimalist syntax*, 243–267. MITWPL, Department of Linguistics and Philosophy, MIT, Cambridge, Mass.

Watanabe, Akira. 1992. WH-in-situ, subjacency, and chain formation. MIT Occasional Papers in Linguistics 2. MITWPL, Department of Linguistics and Philosophy, MIT, Cambridge, Mass.

Watanabe, Akira. 1993. Agr-based Case theory and its interaction with the A-bar system. Doctoral dissertation, MIT, Cambridge, Mass.

Watanabe, Akira. 1995. Conceptual basis of cyclicity. In *MIT working papers in linguistics 27: Papers on minimalist syntax*, 269–291. MITWPL, Department of Linguistics and Philosophy, MIT, Cambridge, Mass.

Webelhuth, Gert. 1989. Syntactic saturation phenomena and the modern Germanic languages. Doctoral dissertation, University of Massachusetts, Amherst.

Whitman, John. 1991. String vacuous V to Comp. Ms., Cornell University, Ithaca, N.Y. [Paper presented at the 14th GLOW Colloquium.]

Zwart, C. Jan-Wouter. 1993. Dutch syntax: A minimalist approach. Doctoral dissertation, University of Groningen.

Index